# You Should Know About the Word of the Lord

Charlene
Altemose, MSC

*Charlene Altemose,*
*M.S.C.*

*May God's Word be your Peace and Joy!*

**Liguori**
ONE LIGUORI DRIVE
LIGUORI MO 63057-9999

Imprimi Potest:
Richard Thibodeau, C.Ss.R.
Provincial, Denver Province
The Redemptorists

ISBN 0-7648-0532-0
Library of Congress Catalog Card Number: 99-66759

To order, call 1-800-325-9521
www.liguori.org
www.catholicbooksonline.com

Cover design by Ross Sherman
Cover photo: Jim and Mary Whitmer

# Contents

# Introduction

The Bible is not only a book in which we find God's presence as we read the Scriptures privately, but it is also the Word of the Lord—a vital part of our communal worship at the liturgy.

Since the Second Vatican Council, the renewal of the liturgy has affected Catholics at the core of our religion. We see the heart and soul of our Catholic faith most clearly when we join with other believers in communal worship.

The renewed liturgy divides our worship into the Liturgy of the Word and the Liturgy of the Eucharist. The Council's document, *The Constitution on the Sacred Liturgy* (Chapter II, 8) encourages the faithful to full participation in the entire Mass, because "the Liturgy of the Word and the Liturgy of the Eucharist...are so closely connected with each other that together they constitute but one single act of worship" (Flannery, 1981).

Like salt and pepper, Gilbert and Sullivan, ham and eggs, so too, Scripture and liturgy are intricately connected. *What You Should Know About the Word of the*

*Lord* is an inspirational guide that spotlights Scripture and liturgy so Catholics can see the correlation between sacred Scripture and its role in the Church's official worship, the Mass. This work facilitates deeper appreciation of Scripture and more meaningful participation in the liturgy, particularly a better understanding of the Liturgy of the Word.

Although Vatican II renewal stresses the Word of the Lord as intimately joined to the Liturgy of the Eucharist, Catholics often find it difficult to see this connection. In addition, they often have difficulty relating the readings of the Mass to their daily life: "Oh, I don't get anything out of the readings, especially the Old Testament" or "I find it hard to see how the readings apply to my life."

Catholics need to see the connection between the lectionary readings, the Eucharist, and personal faith life. To make the Scriptures more alive in our faith life is the primary aim of this volume. It explains the Liturgy of the Word, presents an overview of each book of Scripture, and provides practical guidelines to a more fruitful appreciation of the Word of God.

The Church teaches us that we have four significant encounters with the person of Jesus—in the assembled community, in the Word proclaimed, in the presider, and in the Eucharist. In focusing on the Word proclaimed in liturgy, this book helps the reader see the interconnections among the four ways of encountering Jesus. Like other books in the *What You Should Know About* series, this one has four parts.

Part One discusses the ordinary meaning of *word* as a sharing of one's innermost being with others. So too the Word of God is God's sharing love and concern through the avenue of human words. The more Scripture comes alive for us, the deeper our understanding and appreciation of it. Part One also discusses the significance of the Liturgy of the Word as God's presence to us through the lectionary readings at Mass. It has practical pointers for a more active participation in the readings. This section also describes the roles of the lector and the cantor as well as the purpose and spiritual benefit of the homily.

Part Two explores the Hebrew understanding and experience of God. The author offers a thumbnail sketch of the Hebrew Scriptures (which Christians often call "the Old Testament") and a discussion of the differences between the Protestant and Catholic versions of the Bible. Since the Hebrew Scriptures are often difficult to understand in their context, the author points out the rationale behind scriptural concepts. Part Two also includes suggestions for praying the psalms with faith and devotion. It offers pointers for entering into the spirit of the responsorial psalm.

Part Three considers the Good News of Jesus—his life, mission, and teachings—as presented in the New Testament. This section outlines the stages of development of the gospels, from the disciples' faith experience of Jesus to the written records several decades later. It explores the message and mission of Paul as Apostle to the Gentiles and outlines his letters as vital parts of the New Testament. A discussion of the message and symbolism of the Book of Revelation gives the reader some background to this little-understood book.

Part Four furnishes guidelines for a private praying of the Scriptures as preparation for participation in the Liturgy of the Word. It also considers the liturgical year during which Catholics enter the Paschal Mystery through the Scriptures and liturgy, including the various seasons and the celebration unique to each.

An appendix lists the appropriate readings for each Sunday's liturgy, so that Catholics can resonate with the Scriptures and see the progression of theme in each Sunday's readings. It serves as a handy reference so the reader can prepare ahead and scan the Sunday readings at a glance without paging through a missal or lectionary.

This volume, although not all-encompassing, provides enough information and background that the Liturgy of the Word, personal prayer, and reflections on the Scriptures can be more spiritually enriching. May the reader glean the blessings foretold by Isaiah the prophet:

> *For as the rain and snow come down from heaven,*
> *    and do not return there until they have watered*
> *        the earth,*
> *making it bring forth and sprout,*
> *    giving seed to the sower and bread to the eater,*
> *so shall my word be that goes out from my mouth;*
> *    it shall not return to me empty,*
> *but it shall accomplish that which I purpose,*
> *    and succeed in the thing for which I sent it.*

(Isaiah 55:10-11)

# PART I

# The Word of the Lord

Almost every day we learn of some previously unheard-of form of communication. Cyberspace, internet, fax, and e-mail have become common ways we humans connect and communicate with each other. However, the timeless raw material of all communication is still the human word. We humans could not exist without words, whether written, spoken, or transmitted electronically.

In daily life, words are indispensable for any human interaction. You call to congratulate a friend on an accomplishment. You say good-bye as your child trundles off to school. You tell your beloved of your love. You tune in to the national news. The common element in all these situations is words! What a drab world it would be without the gift of human speech or the dynamism of words.

Think for a moment about the inherent nature of words. Words are magic. They can lift drooping spirits, bolster enthusiasm, make or break a relationship. Words are dynamite and power. They can bring about any desired effect. Words can melt calcified hearts ("I love you"). Words turn despair into hope ("Your test came out negative"). Words too can bring about a catastrophe ("This is a holdup"). Words cement relationships. What joy for parents when their little one's babbling becomes "Dada" and "Mama." A whole new relationship emerges.

Our human ability to communicate in words is a God-given gift. A word reveals the depths of the human heart. When you exchange words with someone, you share what is deep inside you, a part of your inner self, your very soul.

God realized the inherent energy of the human word to make divine love known to all peoples. So through the medium of words, people of all times and all ages came to realize the breadth and width and height and depth of God's love and care for human creatures. The God-experience of the Chosen People and the early Christian community's response to Jesus were cherished in human words, which were passed on to us through remembrance and oral retelling. Later these experiences and revelations were permanently recorded in written form in the sacred Scriptures.

**Revelation of God's Nature and God's Love**

Although the Bible has come down to us in the form of a printed book, it is primarily the record of God's relationship with the Chosen People and with Christ's disciples. In it we read of their faith response to the experience of God and the person of Jesus. That faith response was preserved by individuals who, under the inspiration of the Holy Spirit, recorded in human words how God broke into human history.

The Bible, a record of divine-human interplay, addresses what any relationship demands—discovery, difficulties, change of heart, commitment, and love. The Scriptures depict persons like ourselves, with the same human foibles, hopes, and fears. We meet people who, like us, love, hate, backslide, dream, sin, despair, and hope. In the Bible we also meet noble souls with high degrees of courage, commitment, love, and heroism. Those we meet in the pages of sacred Scripture stand out as prototypes of human reactions, responding to or ignoring God's overtures of love. Despite human shortcomings, God reaches out over and over, loving and caring as only God can.

However, we often relegate the Bible to an obscure niche to collect dust, or we treat it as an ancient text out of touch with modern life. We do not see it as the greatest love story ever told.

We may be repulsed by the backsliding of biblical personalities who in our estimation don't deserve God's care and love. They don't live up to our expectations of what we think they should be. We often expect them to appear in the pages of sacred Scripture with the elegance of figures from a stained-glass window. Yet the people of the Bible are truly human. They are what people everywhere are when they accept or reject God.

God accepts and loves every creature, warts and all. God came to our level to bring us to the divine level, for God made us in the divine image and likeness.

Although the events of the Bible are set in a foreign time and culture, yet we can identify with human behaviors and reactions, for men and women of whatever time and clime have the same needs, aspirations, hopes, and dreams. Human nature is the same the world over and throughout history.

The Bible is not just a frozen collection of tales of the past, God interacting with people of a distant age. We miss the whole purpose of the sacred word when we read the Bible as events happening to people in times long past. The Bible is *our* story, God living today and speaking to us in our day and age. We are Job, Jeremiah, Eve, Ruth, David. We too have rejected the Lord as has Judas. At times we too have put ourselves entirely into the Lord's hands as did Abraham and Moses.

We, like the people of old, are called to the Promised Land. We all have our exoduses and passovers to prepare us for our covenants with and commitment to the Lord. We have our moments when God seems right next to us and those times when we wonder if God knows we exist.

We have times of doubt and despair. We have our sufferings, our days in the desert of spiritual dryness. Every experience that biblical people have in their relationship with God we encounter as well. The Bible truly is relevant to all ages, God speaking to us now.

The Bible, like a mirror, reflects how much God loves us now as in years gone by. We meet the Lord every time we open the Scriptures, whether in private prayer, with others in Bible study groups, or every time we worship together.

We need to get caught up in the drama of the Bible and identify with the people, the saving events, and the divine miracles. Just as God revealed God's self to the Chosen People, God too reveals divine love and care to us through the sacred word, on every page, in every situation. We may not easily get the connection, but at times we can see ourselves and God's work in us with an uncanny, sudden burst of insight. God is so alive in our lives!

The Bible is the avenue through which we can strengthen our love relationship with the Lord. It's when the Lord has broken into our lives, to heal us, to challenge us, to instruct us, to invite us to grow, that we can appreciate the full import of what the Bible really is—God reaching out in love to touch us over and over again.

The Power and Presence of the Lord in the Liturgy

The liturgy of the Mass, the peak of our Catholic faith life, celebrates God's invitation and our response to God's call. We join in the re-enactment of the Paschal Mystery through sacrifice, nourishment, and Christ's sacramental presence. The Word proclaimed, the Eucharist shared, the community of faith assembled, the ordained priest presiding—all show most graphically the presence of Christ among us and the Church as the body of Christ operative in the world today.

In this profound mystery of faith, the Lord invites, shares divine life, and challenges us to be signs of the presence of God. We hear the Word of the Lord and respond to it, we are nourished by the sacramental presence of Christ, and we are called to go forth to be Christ's body in the world. This is the basis and essence of our faith. The Word of the Lord proclaimed in our liturgy aptly prepares us for the challenge.

The Divine Power and Presence in the Liturgy of the Word

Since the renewal of Vatican II, the Liturgy of the Word shares the same status as the Liturgy of the Eucharist—the presence of the Lord among us. The Liturgy of the Word serves as an appropriate preparation for our participation in the Eucharist, and its message enables us to live out our Christian commitment when Mass is over.

The introductory rites of the Liturgy of the Word set the tone for the sacred actions to follow. In many ways these rites resemble the pattern of the Jewish synagogue service—a joyful entrance, welcome, repentance, praise, and prayer. The theme of the liturgy, perhaps read by a commentator before Mass begins, alerts us to the focus of our worship and prepares us to receive the Word. The opening procession, usually composed of the presider and liturgical ministers, publicly witnesses to our unity in faith.

After the presider welcomes the assembly, we make the Sign of the Cross, which affirms our belief in the Trinity and reminds us that Christ's suffering is redemptive. Through the cross, salvation has come to the world, and God's love is made manifest.

We recognize our sinfulness through an act of repentance and the penitential rite. We ask forgiveness of God for personal failures and for our failures as a community of faith to build up the body of Christ in the world.

On some days we recite or sing the Glory to God, an ancient hymn of praise similar to the angels' song at the birth of Christ. (See Luke 2:13-14.)

The opening prayer, formerly called "the collect," gathers the intentions and hopes of the worshiping community. Since we have come from diverse backgrounds and concerns, the opening prayer bonds us together as one community of faith. We join with others in a common faith to honor, praise, and worship God and to be nourished and transformed through the liturgy.

Up to this point, the liturgy has literally lived up to its name, which means "the work of the people." We have addressed God as a single voice in contrition, praise, and unified prayer.

*Immediate Preparation for the Proclamation of the Word*

While the lector proceeds to the ambo or lectern, we prepare for the most important part of the Liturgy of the Word—the proclamation of the Word of God. In the quiet of our hearts, we ask the Lord for an openness to hear the Word.

Proclamation of the Word

The most important part of the Liturgy of the Word is the proclamation of the Word in the lectionary readings and the psalm. The Lord, present in the sacred Word, comes to us and becomes flesh through the proclamation. Although we may be inspired and encouraged by the private reading of Scripture, it has a more dynamic effect when we join with others in worship as a unified people of God, ready and willing to hear and respond to the sacred Word. During the silence between the readings, we savor and internalize the message we have just heard.

*The Lectionary*

The lectionary is the official liturgical book containing passages from the Hebrew Scriptures, the letters, and the gospels that are used during the Mass. The lectionary is positioned on the lectern and opened to the day's readings. The lector proclaims the first and second readings, and sometimes the responsorial psalm, from the lectionary. If the Book of the Gospels (see p. 17) is not used in the Mass, the day's gospel is also proclaimed from the lectionary.

Although the lectionary seems comparable in size to the Bible, the lectionary contains only those Scripture selections that are read during the Liturgy of the Word. The lectionary is divided into two volumes—the Proper of the Seasons for Sundays (years A, B, and C for the three-year Sunday liturgical cycle) and the Proper of the Seasons for Weekdays (years I and II for the two-year cycle of weekday Masses, including the Proper of the Saints). Also included are optional selections that can be chosen for special occasions or specific intentions.

The lector actively assists in bringing the Word to life in the hearts of believers. Through the human voice of the lector, the Word becomes flesh in the midst of the assembly. We become more aware of the Lord's presence when lectors, ministers of the Word, create an environment in which we can more readily experience God.

To proclaim the Scriptures for the worshiping community as a lector is a sacred trust, a challenge that calls for excellence in many ways. Commissioned to be the voice of the Lord, the lector needs to have a passionate love and understanding of the Scriptures. As a person of faith, the lector needs be totally convinced of the sacred mission and so enable the Word of God to come alive in the liturgical assembly through the proclamation.

On Sundays during the year, the first Scripture reading is from the Hebrew Scriptures, except during Eastertime, when the first reading is from the Acts of the Apostles. During Advent the prophet Isaiah dominates. Of the first readings in Advent in cycles A and B, seven are taken from Isaiah. Cycle C features Jeremiah, Baruch, Zephaniah, and Micah. During the Christmas cycle Isaiah is read, except on the feast of the Holy Family, when we hear Sirach 3.

Most of the readings during Lent are stories of how God worked in the history of the Jewish people, in excerpts from Genesis, Exodus, Deuteronomy, Samuel, Chronicles, and Joshua. On the last two Sundays of Lent, passages from the prophets Isaiah, Jeremiah, and Ezekiel are read.

In Ordinary Time, a greater variety of Hebrew Scripture readings are used because of the three-year cycle of the revised liturgy. Even though at Sunday liturgy we do not read from Leviticus, Judges, Ruth, Chronicles, Baruch, Lamentations, Joel, Obadiah, Nahum, Habakkuk, Haggai, and Song of Solomon, some of these are read on weekdays. The Appendix, on page 70, lists the scriptural passages of the Sunday readings for each liturgical cycle.

**The Responsorial Psalm and the Role of the Cantor**

The responsorial psalm serves as a reflective interval in keeping with the theme of the liturgy. Since the psalms contain all human sentiments, the responsorial psalm aptly captures the spirit of the liturgy. The psalm verse is ideally sung by a cantor or choir and the congregation joins with the sung response.

Cantors have always enjoyed a privileged status as vital participants in the Jewish synagogue service, second only to the rabbi. In our revised liturgy, the cantor has entered the mainstream of lay ministers who assist in our worship. As leader of song and chanter of the psalms, the cantor elicits a prayerful response from the people and engages the assembly in a dialogue of praise. The responsorial psalm becomes a vital and significant interchange between God and the people. The cantor mediates this exchange and contributes to a more dynamic worship.

**The Second Reading in Sunday Liturgy**

Because our Christian faith centers on our belief and commitment to the life, message, and mission of Jesus, selections from the New Testament are read at every liturgy. On Sundays and feast days, the second reading, which offers effective ways to put our faith into practice, is from the letters, the Acts of the Apostles, or Revelation.

The second reading each Sunday is usually from the letters of Saint Paul. However, on the Feast of the Baptism of the Lord, we read Acts 10:34-38 and on Christ the King in cycle B, we read Revelation 1:5-8. Some selections from the letters of Peter, John, and Jude are used in weekday Masses.

We affirm the message of the second reading and prepare to hear the gospel with an acclamation. Ordinarily the gospel acclamation consists of a psalm verse, either read or sung, and the sung response of the assembly—an Alleluia, or during Lent with a lenten response, for example, "Praise to you, Lord Jesus Christ." If the response of the assembly is not sung, it is always omitted.

As the proclaimer of the gospel, the presider or any ordained priest prepares to proclaim the gospel with a silent prayer: "Almighty God, cleanse my heart and my lips that I may worthily proclaim your gospel." If a deacon is proclaiming the gospel, he receives a blessing from the presider: "The Lord be in your heart and on your lips that you may worthily proclaim his gospel."

On solemn occasions, the gospel may be read from the Book of the Gospels, which is brought in procession from the altar, accompanied by incense and candles. The Book of the Gospels is then incensed by whomever proclaims the gospel.

Before the gospel is read, the gospel proclaimer traces a Sign of the Cross with his right thumb on the book and on his forehead, lips, and breast. This puts into action the prayer he just silently prayed. As a devotional gesture, we worshipers also trace a cross on our foreheads, lips, and breasts, that the Word of the Lord may be in our minds and hearts and on our lips.

The Gospel Acclamation: Preparation for the Gospel

**Proclamation of the Gospel**

The gospel reading recalls the life, teachings, and healings of Jesus. These selections alternate with the three-year lectionary cycle, so that in the course of three years almost all of each of the gospels is read. Ordinarily the Cycle A gospel is Matthew, Cycle B is Mark, and Cycle C is Luke. John's Gospel is used during the Easter season in all three cycles.

**Solidarity of the Hebrew and Christian Covenants**

During our liturgy we read from both the Hebrew Scriptures and the New Testament to show that God's Covenant with the Jews continues to be a vital part of our Christian faith story and worship. Israel's God-experience forms the foundation on which our faith is based. The revelation to the Jewish people is authentically of God and stands on its own merit as God's self-revelation in the world.

Therefore, in our liturgy, it is fitting that we relive and recall God's working throughout all salvation history, begun with Abraham, continued in Israel's history, and climaxed in the person and message of Jesus.

Jesus confirmed the legitimacy of the Hebrew Covenant: "Do not think that I have come to abolish the law or the prophets; I have come not to abolish, but to fulfill" (Matthew 5:17). Jesus built his teachings and life upon the Hebrew Covenant, perfecting and fulfilling the prophetic promises. Note how often in the gospels and letters we read "as it is written" or "as the prophets foretold." The two readings link our Christian story with the faith of the Jewish people and that of the early Christian Church.

During his visit to the Holy Land, Pope John Paul II affirmed our solidarity with the Jewish people when he begged forgiveness for past injustices against the Jews. To honor the conviction that Christianity is rooted in

Judaism, in this book we call the first part of the Bible "the Hebrew Scriptures," not "the Old Testament."

Do you ever feel that someone isn't tuned in to what you're saying and is a mile away in thought? Do you instinctively react, "You're not with me! Listen to what I'm saying !" It's a natural response to a one-sided communication. You feel like you're talking to a wall. The speaker needs a listener, one who is open and willing to allow the message to get through. Listening is an art that we cultivate so we can concentrate on what the other is sharing with us, because any productive interchange is two-sided. The one who shares needs another with an open, listening heart if the exchange is to be effective.

This is precisely the attitude to foster during the Liturgy of the Word as the Scriptures are proclaimed. God's Word is spoken. So as not to be one-sided, the message must be truly received by attentive, focused listeners. If not, the psalmist's accusation against the rebellious nations will be ours: "They have ears, but do not hear" (Psalm 115: 6).

A word—whether written or spoken—remains dead until it finds a willing, prepared listener. How true this is of the Scriptures and the spirit to which we are called in the Liturgy of the Word! Unless we hear and respond to God's Word, it remains frozen on the page. Listening to the Word of God demands that we give our full attention to the message, however difficult it may sometimes be. Often our own concerns and thoughts block out what is being proclaimed in the readings, or we wander in thought and hardly remember what the readings were. To help you focus better, here are some practical ways you can become actively involved in the symphony of salvation history, played out and recalled at each Sunday liturgy.

1.  Before Mass begins, set your mind upon the sublime act of worship in which you are to participate. Realize you are entering the world of sacred time-space and the divine presence. Leave behind your cares and everyday concerns.

2.  As the commentator reads the introduction and focus of the day, in the quiet of your heart join in spirit with the theme of the liturgy and ask the Lord to spiritually enrich you through the readings and the liturgy with the graces you need.

3.  To profit from Scripture, especially the Hebrew Scriptures, it is good to have a general knowledge of the books of the Bible. The lectionary readings on Sundays link our salvation story with the God-experience of the Jewish people and the Christ-experience of the early Christians. We are not just isolated individuals hearing God's Word; we are significant links between those who preceded us in God's plan and those who will inherit our faith. The Word of God, passed on from generation to generation, speaks to you and me today just as it spoke to our ancestors in the faith.

4.  Learn to see yourself in the lectionary selections, which illustrate God's love for people in all their activities. The stories of the Jewish people represent the gamut of the human condition. We can see ourselves in the wars, violence, and shortcomings as well as in the heroic deeds, commitments, and integrity. We may not experience threats against our lives as they did, but we too wage war against the violence harbored within our own hearts. At times we too allow our best selves to shine forth.

Ask yourself: "How am I like them? Are the prophets speaking to me? How is my situation like theirs? Am I as unfaithful in my duties as the shortcomings I hear of in Scripture?" The Bible is a mirror. See your image there. Realize the Lord used the ancient nomadic culture to break into human history. Try to understand the environment of the times, so you can see the universality of human need. Allow the Lord to work in your heart, breaking into your heart with the same compassion, love, and concern God has for all people. Join in spirit with God's working in the hearts of the Jewish people as the Hebrew Scriptures are proclaimed.

When we empathize with all human beings, including our Jewish forebears, and understand their situation, we will not label the Hebrew Scriptures "old and outdated." Instead we acknowledge God continuing to work anew in our midst through the sacred words as they come alive here and now in our worshiping assembly.

5. During the responsorial psalm, join your prayer with the pleas and cries of the Jewish people. The psalms speak of concerns deep within the human heart. The prayers of the psalmist are ours. The responsorial psalm provides an appropriate time to lift up our cares to the Lord. Thus united with others in worship, our burdens become lighter because others are praying for us, too. We respond to the responsorial psalm in a spirit of openness and dependence on God. Although our personal feelings may not resonate today with the sentiments expressed in a particular psalm, we remember that at liturgy our voices and prayers embrace the whole human family. We think of those

for whom this responsory is an earnest, heartfelt plea, and we offer our prayerful support.

6. The second reading usually contains practical advice on living out our Christian call. Picture yourself seated at the feet of the apostle-author. Imagine that his advice is addressed to you, and make the message your own. How can you put it into practice and improve in your Christian life? When a passage speaks directly to you, hold on to it and use it during the day as a prayerful reminder. Enflesh the Word of the Lord, making it truly alive in your own life.

7. As you prepare to hear the gospel message, enthusiastically join in the gospel acclamation, conscious of Christ's presence soon to be proclaimed. Trace the sign of the cross on your forehead, lips, and breast that you may hear what the Lord knows you need to hear. If any passage strikes you personally, thank God for the awareness, and savor the inspiration.

8. Listen to each gospel reading as addressed to you so you may actually hear the Lord speaking to you personally. Relive the event presented in the gospel. In the spirit of Saint Ignatius Loyola, put yourself in the gospel scene. As you listen and respond to the Scriptures, ask yourself, "What is the Lord saying to me now?" "How can I live out the ideals that Jesus teaches?" Although the gospels are the most familiar parts of Scripture, when you are attentive and focused, you may really hear the gospel in a different light. When the words of Scripture hit "right between the eyeballs," we realize the Lord is saying something important to us personally.

9. As you hear the words, focus and pay attention. To really listen requires effort, especially at a crowded

Sunday liturgy, where there are often many distractions. If you read over the passages before Mass, then when the words are proclaimed, you can more easily focus and listen with your heart, body, mind, and spirit. As many times as you become distracted—and some days are much worse than others—gently call your attention back. Even great saints struggled at times with distractions.

The reading of the Scriptures during the liturgy is the time we as a worshiping community hear God speaking to each of us. For God knows the inmost heart of everyone and speaks to each heart as only God knows how. To be attentive is to glean from the Word the rich spiritual gifts meant especially for you. The message of the Scriptures amplified by the homilist may provide even further spiritual nourishment and stimulation for leading a more God-focused life.

The homily, delivered either by the presider, another priest, or a deacon, follows the gospel. This was formerly referred to as a "sermon," but since liturgical renewal it is called a "homily," a less formal term, from Greek, which means a "conversation with the people." The challenging role of the homilist is to break open the Word, to present for reflection some uplifting and challenging message and relate the Scripture readings to our daily lives. A good homily moves us to live the Scriptures in our own lives; it "comforts the afflicted but also afflicts the comfortable." Blessed are those congregations whose homilist can apply the Scriptures to life in a meaningful, creative way and facilitate the transition from the proclaimed Word to a faith in action.

**The Role of the Homily**

**Listening to the Homily Creatively**

How do you listen to a homily creatively? High on my pet-peeve list is a long, drawn-out homily poorly delivered. I have heard thousands of homilies in my life, and one way I have overcome my annoyance with shoddy homilies is to make up my own as I listen to the reading. Instead of fuming and being irritated, I ask myself, *What motif and message can I take with me? What is the Lord saying to me today? What message would I deliver if I were to give the homily?* This has helped me be more attentive, but also it makes the Word of the Lord more relevant to my situation. I select one word or passage as the prayer word of my day, a short passage that I learn by heart that prods me to remember the Lord's word to me.

Often when we hear a challenging homily we are tempted to think, "If only so-and-so would hear this." It's easier to see how the homily fits someone else than it is to see how it applies to us. It's precisely what our Lord warned against: "Why do you see the speck in your neighbor's eye, but do not notice the log in your own eye?" (Matthew 7:3). Next time you hear a homily, try to make it creative. Ask yourself, *What would I say?*

**The Nicene Creed: Our Profession of Faith**

After we hear the Word of God proclaimed and we reflect on the message at the homily, we stand and publicly profess our common faith. The Nicene Creed, sung or recited in unison, expresses our acceptance of the main truths of our faith and our witness to it. First formulated at the Council of Nicaea in A.D. 325 for use at baptisms, the Nicene Creed provides an opportunity for us to renew our baptismal vows and our commitment to the Catholic way of life.

The general intercessions or prayer of the faithful concludes the Liturgy of the Word. Because we are one in the Spirit, we need to express in the intentions a strong sense of solidarity with others through a global concern. We open our hearts in prayer for the Church, civil authority, the whole human family, and our own community. The presider begins the intercessions with an invitation to join in prayer. The deacon or lector reads or chants the petitions to which the congregation responds with a brief plea, such as, "Lord, hear our prayer." We enlarge our horizons and reach out in compassion and empathy, readying ourselves to approach the Eucharist united in hope and prayer for the whole human family. An effective silent pause at the end of the intercessions provides an opportunity for us to place our personal needs before the Lord in prayer.

Now that the Liturgy of the Word has ended, we are prepared to unite with Christ in the perfect gift to the Father, Jesus' own Body and Blood under the appearances of bread and wine.

For a detailed explanation of and information about the entire liturgy, see *What You Should Know About the Mass*, by Charlene Altemose, MSC.

The General Intercessions: Conclusion of the Liturgy of the Word

# The Hebrew Scriptures

## (*Old Testament*)

The
Hebrew
Scriptures:
God's
Saving
Action in
History

O n Sundays and feast days when three lectionary passages are read, the first selection is usually from the Hebrew Scriptures because Jews and Christians share in the heritage of Abraham—belief in one God and in God's saving action in history. The Hebrew Scriptures form the foundation of our Christian faith, which did not develop in a vacuum. Many Christian traditions and liturgical practices are an outgrowth of Judaism. Remember, Jesus was a practicing Jew. God's revelation to the Jews is as relevant to Christians today as it was to people in biblical times.

The Hebrew Scriptures are ancient, developed long before the printing press. Most of the content was first transmitted by word of mouth. Later it was recorded on papyrus scrolls with reed instruments. This is hard to understand for those raised with pens, paper, typewriters, and computers. Before we delve into the individual books of the Hebrew Scriptures, consider how ancient civilizations perceived reality and how observation of nature and experience formed their world view.

Long ago, when the human family was quite young and before any records were kept, the ancient peoples, left to their imagining, groped for an understanding of the power that ruled the world, things over which we humans have no control. Very early they found out that the human being is limited. The world is full of mysteries that humans cannot comprehend. To make sense out of life and to discover more about the mysterious, they devised ways to placate and honor this power. Through reasoning and logic, they concluded that the universe is dominated by unseen forces. Each civilization and people, attempting to cope with life's baffling mysteries, created a variety of gods, myths, and rituals in a specific way that we call "religion."

How did the ancient Jewish people come to the understanding of one God? Why was Yahweh so significant in their lives when other peoples had myriads of gods and spirits in their religious beliefs? God realized the human heart could not relate to an abstract deity through reasoning and logic alone.

**The Jewish Understanding of One God**

So at a certain point in history, around 1850 B.C., the patriarch Abraham came to realize that this overriding presence was one and personal. In Abraham's daily life, this power revealed love and concern.

Abraham found that this power ruled his life. With faith in the Lord, Abraham abandoned his comfortable existence in Haran and headed south to Canaan, the land to which God called him. This is the beginning of the saga of the one God. Abraham discovered that the supreme power that governed the universe was one with whom we could relate on a personal level.

This ancient people's experiences of and response to the one God, as well as God's reaching out and guiding them, make up the raw material of the Hebrew Scriptures. The Jews came to realize that every aspect of their lives was governed by this One whom they called "Lord." Their lives took shape in response to the Covenant they made through Abraham and Moses. Prophets kept reminding them of their pact with the Infinite. God was very real to the Jewish people, a conviction and belief passed on from the time of Abraham. Each event that happened to them was attributed to the one personal God. They developed their moral system, fought wars, and made treaties according to the will of God. Memory and storytelling were their basic communication tools. Later they collated and preserved this memory of God's saving events in the Hebrew Scriptures.

What Christians call "the Old Testament" is the response of the Jewish people to the Covenant—their remembered history, hymns and prayers, stories, teachings, and the prophets' exhortations. No matter what literary style or form is used, one thread is woven through the whole of the Hebrew Scriptures: God is one who acts in history and who made a Covenant with the people.

**Christians and the Hebrew Scriptures**

Christians look at the Hebrew Scriptures as the beginning of God's revelation of divine love, which we believe culminated in the coming of Christ, who is the ultimate revelation of divine love. The Hebrew Scriptures are not a scaffold that we discard because Jesus came. The Hebrew Scriptures are the foundation and bedrock of faith. Jesus was born into the way of life, spiritual outlook, faith, and culture shaped by the Hebrew

Scriptures. He was—first and foremost—a devout Jew. Does it surprise you? Jesus was not a Christian!

Christian rituals did not begin in a vacuum, but developed from Jewish concepts. Much of what we do in our Christian and Catholic rituals is rooted in Jewish practices. For example, the entire Liturgy of the Word is patterned after the Jewish synagogue service. And at the beginning of the Liturgy of the Eucharist, the Prayer for the Preparation of the Altar and the Gifts, "Blessed are you, Lord, God of all creation. Through your goodness we have this bread to offer," is a Jewish blessing, a *berakhah*.

Because the Hebrew Scriptures are a product of a different age and culture, Catholics sometimes find it difficult to relate to the readings and make sense of Hebrew Scripture passages. To grasp the significance of the Hebrew Scriptures better, we can use the following Jewish concepts to help us appreciate the foundations laid in the Jewish faith and relevant to Christians today.

## The Jewish Concept of God and the Human Response

The mysteries of the universe and the world of the unseen and unknown became real for the Jewish people through their faith in one God who was personally involved in their history. God for the Chosen People was one who governed every aspect of their lives. To respond to God was to obey the laws they believed came directly from God.

Because all their actions flowed from God's law and were their response to direct commands from God, the Hebrew Scriptures are filled with "The Lord said.…" Browse through the Book of Leviticus to get an idea that every aspect of life was regulated by laws. Because God was their supreme ruler, the Jewish people attributed all their fortunes or misfortunes to their fidelity or infidelity to the Covenant and the laws.

## The Jewish Understanding of Life and Time

Unlike those who often fail to recognize the sacred in the world, devout Jews saw God in every aspect of creation. Everything was fingerprinted by the divine hand. The beauty of the universe did not detract from God but pointed to God's creative love. When observing something that gave delight or joy, the Jew pronounced a *berakhah*, a blessing: "Blessed are you, Lord, king of the universe who has given me...."

The Jewish people did not attempt to explain the change of seasons or rhythms of nature scientifically but saw all as part of God's creation. They ritually celebrated with holy days and festivals. They held Sabbath as a day of rest in imitation of the Creator who rested on the seventh day. Their festivals recalled the times when God dramatically guided them, especially Passover. The lunar cycles held particular fascination. As the first sliver of the new moon appeared, the Jews observed a festival of the new moon.

## The Hebrew Mentality and Concept of History

The Hebrew understanding of history is unlike the modern Western notion. History for us is dates, times, places, and specific persons. The Hebrew understanding of history is much less accurate according to our standards.

In the eighteenth century, Western historical efforts came under the influence of scientific reasoning and methods. Since then, dates, numbers, and exactness of data are crucial in recording events. We are concerned with accuracy. We ask, "Did it really happen that way?"

On the other hand, ancient peoples were not as concerned with accurate data as with symbolic meanings.

The Hebrews asked, "What does it mean?" This distinction between our culture and that of the Hebrews is important to remember as we read the Hebrew Scriptures.

The stories of the Hebrew Scriptures are recorded for their purpose and deeper meaning. So do not let a desire for accurate ages, years, and numbers hinder your appreciation of the Scriptures. Avoid getting hung up on trivial data or logical questioning.

## The Role of Oral Storytelling and Tradition

Recall the childhood game called "Whispering Down the Alley" or "Telephone"? The first child whispered something to the next one, and it was passed on. By the time the secret got to the end of the line, it had changed considerably. Oral tradition, passed on from generation to generation, is like that. It changes form and substance, although the main idea may remain. Almost all of the Hebrew Scriptures were originally passed on by word of mouth, although some things may have been committed to writing in the early stages, for example, the Ten Commandments, court annals, or laws. So in reading the Hebrew Scriptures, remember that they are primarily a written record of an oral tradition. Hence, discrepancies and conflicting accounts abound.

## Concept of Community and Group Mentality

The people of Israel were a community-based society. Their main concern was the welfare of the group. A person was not merely an individual but a vital part of the clan or tribe. Such corporate understanding is hard for us to grasp in our age of individualism. When individual persons are mentioned in the Hebrew Scriptures, it is always in the context of community.

The nomadic way of life necessitated dependence and reliance on each other. It was unheard of to consider life apart from the group. They lived in community, worshiped in community, and were governed by the community. The preservation of their history and record of God's dealings with them was determined by the group.

Although certain persons were commissioned to commit their history to writing, the Scriptures were developed as a group endeavor to preserve and pass on their heritage. We need to understand and judge all we read in the Hebrew Scriptures according to this corporate or tribal mindset.

## What About All the Wars and Violence?

One difficult problem Christians have with the Hebrew Scriptures is that the wars and violence seem to contradict the notion of the Jews as God's Chosen People.

Remember, we are dealing with the cultural patterns and ways of ancient peoples. They believed that wars between peoples were a result of wars between cosmic powers, between their gods and other gods. Since the Jews believed in the utter oneness and holiness of God, anyone who did not believe in their God was to be punished. We find this attitude harsh and contrary to our values. However, a Hebrew's moral standards were based on the conviction that victories and losses, successes and failures in life depended on fidelity or infidelity to the Covenant with God.

## Names of the People in the Hebrew Scriptures

The Jewish people are referred to in a number of ways in their sacred writings. In the sojourn in Egypt they are called "Hebrews," which means "people from across the river." After the Covenant with God on Mount Sinai, they are called "the Chosen People," not because of favoritism on the part of God but because they recognized the supreme power as one and personal.

Later they are called "Israelites" because when they settled in the land of Canaan, they were all descendants of Jacob, whose name had been changed to Israel. After the Exile in 537 B.C., Judah was the only tribal territory that survived, and so they were called "Jews," a term still used.

Ancient people knew nothing of plagiarism or copyright. All life was lived in togetherness. So the Scriptures, although finally written by individuals, were formed from the memory of the group. We cannot pinpoint authorship to one individual. However, the Jewish people often gave author credit to a specific figure. For example, Moses is called the author of the Torah or Pentateuch, the first five books of the Hebrew Scriptures. David is looked upon as the author of the Psalms. Solomon is credited with the Song of Songs, which is also known as the Song of Solomon.

## Authorship of the Hebrew Bible

In the nineteenth century, scholars began to examine the Scriptures critically. While noting historical and textual discrepancies and literary features, they discovered that oral traditions were passed on in various strains and later woven together as a whole. The ancient Hebrews were not so much concerned with accuracy as they were with significance, the deeper meaning of their faith story. As we read through the Hebrew Scriptures, we may discover repetitions and conflicting information. For example, read the first two chapters of Genesis, and compare the details of the two creation accounts.

## Variant Traditions

Basic to understanding the Hebrew Scriptures is to determine what genre or literary form is used. Just as you read each section of the daily newspaper with a different mindset, you need to ask how the Jews expressed their experience of God in the various literary forms.

## The Books of the Hebrew Scriptures

Is it an historical recording of events as they occurred? Is it a prophet's admonition to a certain king, comment on a specific issue, or foretelling of impending doom? Is it a prayer used in the pilgrimage to Jerusalem, or a psalm sung in the Temple? Is it a story of a person who actually lived, or is it a parable told to get a point across? Is it a story told and retold, embellished as it went along in the oral tradition?

## The Differences Between the Catholic and Protestant Canons

The Jewish Bible and the Protestant Hebrew Scriptures each include thirty-nine books. The Catholic version of the Hebrew Scriptures has forty-six books. There is a simple explanation for this discrepancy. After the Exile, 587 to 537 B.C., some Jews returned to Jerusalem. As they continued practicing their faith and traditions, they compiled their collective experience of God in sacred writings, which came to be known as the Palestinian canon.

Many Jews also settled in Alexandria, Egypt. Although Greek was their customary language and culture, they wished to uphold their Jewish religion but could not understand the Hebrew. So around 270 B.C. the Hebrew Scriptures were translated into Greek. Included in this version, known as the Septuagint, were seven books not included in the Hebrew Scriptures. These are Tobit, Judith, 1 and 2 Maccabees, Baruch, Wisdom, and Sirach. So from there on, two versions of the Jewish Bible existed—the Hebrew version called the Palestinian canon (*canon* means *a list of accepted books*) and the Alexandrian canon or Septuagint, which is the Greek translation with the seven additional books, which are collectively called "the Apocrypha."

In A.D. 390 Pope Damasus assigned Saint Jerome to translate the Scriptures into Latin, the language of the

Church. Jerome used the Septuagint version to translate the Scriptures into Latin. This translation is called the Vulgate, from a word meaning *language of the people*. Because the Vulgate included the seven books of the Greek canon that were not in the Hebrew version, this longer version became the official inspired Word of God and Bible of the Church, along with the New Testament.

In A.D. 1517 Martin Luther advocated the translation of the Bible into the current language of the people. A Scripture scholar and linguist, Luther used the Hebrew Palestinian canon to translate the Bible into German. This version, minus the seven books of the Alexandrian canon, became the official Bible of the Protestant churches.

For this reason, since the Reformation there has been a discrepancy between the Protestant and Catholic Bibles. Today Protestant Bibles include the seven books as "Apocrypha," added after the thirty-nine books. Catholic Bibles include the seven books within the text.

As you compare various Bibles, you will notice that names might be spelled differently. This, too, can be explained. Variant spellings of proper names depend on whether the Hebrew spelling or Greek spelling is used. Today most Bibles revert to the Hebrew spelling for greater uniformity. Some names with very different spellings include Hosea (Osee), Ezra (Esdras), Obadiah (Abdiah) and Joshua (Josue). The prophets usually end in *-ah* in Hebrew and *-a* in Greek, for example, Isaiah (Isaia).

**Variant Names of the Books**

# HISTORY OF THE JEWISH PEOPLE: A TIME LINE

## PREHISTORY
Gn. 1—11

**B.C.**

## PATRIARCHAL AGE
*1850 – 1300*

| 1850 | 1700 – 1300 |
|---|---|
| Call of Abraham Gn. 12 | Isaac, Jacob, Joseph Gn. 25—50 |
| | Sojourn in Egypt Ex. 1 |

## EXODUS & CONQUEST OF PALESTINE
*1300 – 1000*

| 1300 | 1250 – 1000 |
|---|---|
| Call of Moses Ex., Lev., Nm., Dt. | Joshua enters Palestine Jos. |
| | Period of the Judges Jgs. |

## UNITED KINGDOM
*1000 – 922 BC*

| c. 1000 | 970 | 940 – 922 | 922 |
|---|---|---|---|
| Saul 1 Sm. 9—15 | David 1 Sm. 16— 2 Sm. 10 1 Chr. 3—29 | Solomon 1 Kgs. 1—11 2 Chr. 1—9 | Split into Kingdom of Judah and Kingdom of Israel 1 Kgs. 11, 14 2 Chr. 11 |

## THE KINGDOM DIVIDED
*922 BC – 587 BC*

| 922 | 722 | 587 |
|---|---|---|
| | Assyrians Capture Israel 1 Kgs. 12— 2 Kgs. 17 | Babylon Captures Judah 1 Kgs. 12— 2 Kgs. 17 2 Chr. 10—36 |

## BABYLONIAN EXILE
*587 – 537*

| 587 | — | 537 |
|---|---|---|
| Exile Ez., Jer. Is. 40—55 2 Kgs. 24—25 | | |

## PERSIAN ERA
*537 – 333*

| 537 | 333 |
|---|---|
| Hebrews return to Palestine Ez., Neh. 1 Mc. 1 | Alexander the Great conquers Palestine 1 Mc. 1 |

## GREEK ERA
*333 – 63*

| 333 | 175 – 135 | 134 |
|---|---|---|
| | Maccabees revolt 1, 2 Mc. | Hasmonean Rulers |

## ROMAN RULE
*63 B.C. – ca. A.D. 300*

| 63 – 37 | 37 – 4 | ca. 4 | A.D. 37 – 44 | 44 – 66 | 66 – 70 |
|---|---|---|---|---|---|
| Jewish High Priests Rule | Herod the Great | Birth of Jesus | Herod Agrippa | Roman Procurators | Revolt — Destruction of Temple |

**Jewish Diaspora—Jews scattered.** *Early dates are approximate. This represents a history of the Jewish people only. The Christian era overlaps and is outlined in Part Three.*

The first five books of the Bible are especially revered by the Jewish people as the written Law of Moses, the Torah, a Hebrew word meaning *to instruct*. Later these were called "the Pentateuch," a Greek word meaning *five volumes*. These books contain the laws and the Covenant God made with the Jewish people through Moses. These laws were the first parts of the Hebrew Scriptures committed to writing. Later, after the Exile, the collected stories of the patriarchs Abraham, Isaac, Jacob, and Joseph were compiled. Although Abraham (c.1850) was the first patriarch, he was not the first human being. This consideration led the Jewish people to speculate about human origins. Modeling their explanation on the Babylonian myths of creation, the Jewish writers wanted to show the power and oneness of their God and to explain how and why sin came into the world. Thus, sometime during and after the Exile, they compiled the first eleven chapters of Genesis as explanation of human beginnings and the human condition, according to their understanding of God.

**GENESIS**–The first eleven chapters record ancient times before history was written. These chapters tell of creation, Adam and Eve, Cain and Abel, and Noah. They present genealogies and theological explanations of the world and sin. Chapters 12 to 50 relate the stories of the patriarchs—Abraham, Isaac, Jacob, and Joseph. These are family stories passed on orally. Repetitions and discrepancies exist because one account was woven from several traditions.

**EXODUS**–This is the story of Moses and the people leaving Egypt enroute to the Promised Land. It tells of their

*Books in the Hebrew Bible*

*The Torah*

forty-year sojourn in the desert, the Covenant, and the Ten Commandments.

**LEVITICUS**–Leviticus emphasizes that commitment to a Covenant with Yahweh demands obedience to the many laws that governed every aspect of life. It outlines the duties of the priests and prescribes the Temple sacrifices and festivals.

**NUMBERS**–This book is so named because of the census numbers that figure prominently. It also records the Israelites' forty-year sojourn in the desert, the conquest of territory along the way, and preparations for conquest of the Promised Land, with Joshua as Moses' successor.

**DEUTERONOMY**–Deuteronomy, which means *the second law,* is an expansion of the laws found in Exodus. The themes throughout Deuteronomy include the Jewish theology of one God, one land, and one people. It ends with the last testament and death of Moses and the commissioning of Joshua.

*Historical Books or Early Prophets*

In the Hebrew Bible, the books of Joshua, Judges, Ruth, and Kings are called "Early Prophets," while in the Greek and Christian Bibles these are referred to as "Historical Books," along with Chronicles, Ezra, Nehemiah, Tobit, Judith, Esther, and the two books of the Maccabees. These books are historical because they deal with the life and events of the people of Israel.

**JOSHUA**–The book of Joshua tells of the people's entrance into the Promised Land under the leadership of Joshua. It describes the conquest and division of the land among the tribes of Jacob, up until the death of Joshua around 1200 B.C.

**JUDGES**–After the death of Joshua, there is no central authority. The people are under judges who lead a tribe or several tribes. Most well-known among the judges include Gideon, Samson, and Deborah. Historically, the judges prevailed until the kingship of Saul, around 1000 B.C. While the Book of Joshua makes the conquest appear miraculous and easy, the Book of Judges shows how the people fought to capture the land.

**RUTH**–A lovely story of David's great-grandmother, a Moabite woman, a widowed foreigner, who stays with her mother-in-law, Naomi, and becomes a faithful believer in Yahweh.

*The Kings*

The books of Samuel, Kings, and Chronicles record the reigns of the kings in both the united and the divided kingdom of Israel until the fall of Jerusalem in 587 B.C. They are not strictly chronological but are collections of stories showing how Israel prospered or failed depending on fidelity to Yahweh.

**1 SAMUEL**–Samuel, the last judge, anoints Saul as the first king around 1000 B.C. This book contains the story of the famous bout between David and Goliath and David's subsequent anointing as the second king around 970 B.C.

**2 SAMUEL**–David reigns as king and establishes Jerusalem as the capital. Included are David's family history, his military prowess, his sins and failures, and the court annals of his reign.

**1 KINGS**–The death of David is followed by the reign of Solomon, which began in splendor with the building of the Temple. But wealth, fame, and power caused Solomon's downfall. After Solomon's death in 922 B.C., the kingdom is split. The northern ten tribes become Israel and the southern part is Judah.

**2 KINGS**–Assyria, Babylon, and Egypt vie for control of the Chosen People's land. In 722 B.C. Assyria captures the north. The kingdom of Judah lasts until 587 B.C. when the Babylonians conquer Jerusalem and take the Jews captive. The captivity in Babylon lasts until 537 B.C. when the Babylonians are captured by the Persians who allow the Jews to return home.

**1 AND 2 CHRONICLES**–The Chronicles retell the Jewish history of Samuel and the kings in an idealized manner. The Chronicles contain genealogies and describe the temple worship. Although repetitions and discrepancies abound, the stories reveal God's active role in Jewish history.

*Post-Exilic Books: Ezra and Nehemiah*

The books of Ezra and Nehemiah record how God fulfills the promise for the people to return to Jerusalem. They also recount restoring a Jewish community after the Exile, from 537 B.C. until about 444 B.C.

**EZRA**–The Book of Ezra tells of the rebuilding of the Temple by Zerubabel through the encouragement and promptings of the prophets Haggai and Zechariah. Ezra, a scribe learned in the Mosaic Law and Torah, brings about religious renewal and rekindles Jewish fervor.

**NEHEMIAH**–Nehemiah is commissioned by the King of Persia to oversee the return of the Jews from captivity. He rebuilds the walls of Jerusalem, takes a census, abolishes abuses, and leads the people to recommit themselves to the Lord.

**POST-EXILIC STORIES**–Included in the Catholic Bible are three post-exilic stories. Tobit, Judith, and Esther are not necessarily historical figures, but the tales can be classed as religious fiction, stories told to teach a lesson or drive home a point.

**TOBIT**–The story of Tobit is told for Jews who, after the exile, worried about whether they could be faithful Jews amid an alien culture. Tobit and his family, deported to Assyria, prove they can remain faithful to Yahweh. God provides care through the angel Raphael, who accompanies young Tobit on his journey to collect a debt owed his father. He returns with a beautiful wife, Sarai. The elder Tobit is rewarded for his goodness by being healed of his blindness.

**JUDITH**–Judith, a young Hebrew girl, beguiles the enemy leader, Holofernes, with her charms, cuts off his head, and thus saves Israel from attack by the Assyrians.

**ESTHER**–Esther is the story of a heroic Jewish woman who becomes the queen of King Xerxes (485 B.C.). Her uncle Mordecai, a devout Jew, displeases Haman, a court official, who decides to get rid of all Jews. Esther pleads with the king, Mordecai is saved, and Haman is executed. To this day, Jews celebrate their survival and God's providence in the festival of Purim. They reenact the story of

Esther and feast on a special pastry called hamantashen, symbolic of the triangular hat worn by Haman.

**1 MACCABEES**–Named after Judas Maccabeus, the son of Mattathias, the books of the Maccabees recount the upholding of Jewish traditions and their battles against the persecutions of the Seleucid ruler Antiochus IV in 167 B.C.

**2 MACCABEES**–This book aims to strengthen Jewish faith by upholding as heroic those who suffered persecution for the faith, especially the story of Eleazar and the mother with her seven sons, who endured death rather than be disloyal to their faith.

The Festival of Hanukkah, recorded in 2 Maccabees 10:1-8, observed by Jews even to this day, commemorates the rededication of the Temple in 164 B.C. when the oil, enough for only one day, miraculously continued to burn for eight days.

*Wisdom Books*     In the Hebrew Scriptures, Job, Psalms, Proverbs, Ecclesiastes, and Song of Solomon are referred to as "The Writings." Because these deal with issues of life and the handling of life situations, in the Greek canon they are called "Wisdom Literature," along with the books of Wisdom and Sirach.

**JOB**–Job is probably the most popular and well-known personality of the Hebrew Scriptures. However, the story of Job is meant to teach a lesson, not necessarily tell the story of a person who actually lived. The narrative sets the scene in which a good and pious man loses everything in life. The bulk of the text concerns the dialogues between Job and his three friends who taunt and cajole him as he confronts the mystery of good and evil in the world. This story attempts to answer why "bad things happen to good people."

**PSALMS**–In every Bible, the Psalms are positioned between Job and Proverbs, but they are treated in greater detail at the end of this chapter, because of their importance in the Liturgy of the Word.

**PROVERBS**–Proverbs is a down-to-earth collection of pithy sayings and sage advice. Proverbs 31 extols the virtues of a good woman and is used in Jewish households at the Sabbath meal.

**ECCLESIASTES**–This book opens with the image of a cynic, Qoheleth, who is decrying the futility of life: "Vanity of vanities!" He is challenged by the mystery of good and evil and wonders what is the use of it all. Along with Job, Ecclesiastes is called "Problem Literature," because these books wrestle with the hard questions of life. A much-quoted passage, Ecclesiastes 3:1-8, reflects on the meaning of time: "For everything there is a season, and a time for every matter under the sun."

**SONG OF SOLOMON**–A love poem, this book extols the beauty of the love relationship between a man and a woman as comparable to God's love for us.

**WISDOM**–The Book of Wisdom was written around 100 B.C. by a Jew who had been influenced by Greek thinking and culture. Originally written in Greek, it is not included in the Hebrew Scriptures. The author praises the sublime nature of true wisdom as being rooted in

God. The author also recalls for the Jews how God stood by them in all the saving events of their history.

**SIRACH**–Originally written in Hebrew, this book was taken to Egypt and included in the Greek canon. It is a collection of proverbs, sayings, and common-sense advice topically arranged. Because it was widely used in the early Church, it became known as "Ecclesiasticus," or "the Church Book."

*The Prophetic Books*    The prophetic books include the four major (Isaiah, Jeremiah, Ezekiel, Daniel) and the twelve minor prophets of the Jewish people. In addition, the books of Lamentations and Baruch, connected with the prophet Jeremiah, are considered separate books.

**ISAIAH**–The Book of Isaiah, the best-known and most-quoted of the prophetic books, is named for Isaiah, a prophet in Jerusalem around 740 B.C. He is the "prophet of the holiness of God" who called for reform at a time of moral decline. Chapters 1-39 are attributed to Isaiah, while chapters 40-66 were written during and after the Exile.

**JEREMIAH**–Jeremiah lamented over Jerusalem before its destruction in 587 B.C. and was carried into exile in Egypt. His prophecies are full of woe and sorrow.

**LAMENTATIONS**–A selection of wailings about the destruction of the Temple, this book is connected to Jeremiah.

**BARUCH**–The Book of Baruch, not in the Hebrew canon, is attributed to Baruch, a follower of Jeremiah. Probably addressed to Jews during the Babylonian captivity, it offers prayers of hope for deliverance and praises the wisdom of the Law of Moses. It concludes with a letter Jeremiah wrote to the captives warning against idolatry.

**EZEKIEL**–Ezekiel is the prophet of the Exile. He kept alive their hope while in Exile in Babylon. Through vivid imagery and symbol, Ezekiel shows God is still with them. We remember Ezekiel especially for the image of dry bones in chapter 37.

**DANIEL**–The Book of Daniel is a mixture of wondrous miracles and prophetic imagery. Its hero is Daniel, a young Jewish man, brought to work in the Babylonian palace. Thrown into the lion's den for defying the king's order, Daniel is preserved from harm. The author uses the apocalyptic form, which through symbols, visions, and numbers, sends the message that God protects those who are faithful.

**HOSEA**–A prophet of the northern kingdom around 750 B.C., Hosea foresees Hebrew infidelity and speaks of Yahweh's love for Israel. Hosea uses touching imagery of a loving parent fondling a child to illustrate God's love for Israel.

**JOEL**–After the Exile, Joel uses a locust plague as symbol of impending doom. He prophesies of the "Day of the Lord" when the fullness of God's Spirit will be poured out, a passage used in the Pentecost liturgy.

**AMOS**–A Judean shepherd, Amos speaks out against social injustices and evils to the kings of the north, 760 B.C.

**OBADIAH**–As the shortest book of the Hebrew Scriptures, Obadiah prophesies the destruction that will come upon Edom, a nation hostile to the Jewish people.

**JONAH**–The Book of Jonah is the parable of a prophet, not necessarily a historic figure, called by God to preach repentance to Nineveh, the enemy. He refuses to go and is swallowed by a big fish who spews him onto the land of Nineveh. It's a far cry from reality but gets the point across: God calls even those we consider enemies. Written at a time when Jews thought they had a monopoly on God's goodness, it teaches of God's providence and care for all peoples.

**MICAH**–Micah, a contemporary of Isaiah, challenges people to faithful observance of the Law.

**NAHUM**–Nahum sees the destruction of Assyria's Nineveh in 612 B.C. as God's vengeance for their evil ways.

**HABAKKUK**–Habakkuk cries out against the evils rampant all around. He questions why evil persists and that the good suffer at the hands of evildoers.

**ZEPHANIAH**–Zephaniah deplores pagan worship and warns of the approach of the "Day of the Lord."

**HAGGAI**–After the exile, Haggai reminds the people of their religious duties and their promise to rebuild the Temple.

**ZECHARIAH**–Zechariah calls the people to repent, observe the Law, and renew their faith by rebuilding the Temple.

**MALACHI**–After the Temple is rebuilt, Malachi deplores the abuses that have inched their way into Temple worship (c. 450 B.C.).

The Book of Psalms, a collection of one hundred fifty prayers, proclaims God's praise and deeds in poetry and song. They were used primarily in Temple worship and in pilgrimage. In other books of the Bible, God reveals the divine presence through events and persons. But in the psalms, the human heart reaches out in pursuit of God. The psalms relate neither story nor events but speak the language of a special relationship of Israel with God. Because God was accessible and approachable, the Jewish people expressed all their needs, anxieties, and hopes in sincere prayer.

*The Psalms: Prayer Book and Hymnal of the Jewish People*

The psalms embrace all sentiments of the human heart. As you scan the psalms, notice how, like an emotional roller-coaster, you skip from joy and exultation to utter despair and frustration. Such is the human heart—mercurial and changeable. There is a psalm for every reason, every season, every sentiment. The psalms are the prayers of everyone.

When you express deep feelings, it is not hard to wax eloquent or become poetic. Think of the flowery language lovers use to articulate their affections. So the psalms are rife with images, symbols, and beautiful poetry. To resonate with them, we need to understand how the Chosen People experienced God. In expressing this relationship, they saw God in every part of creation. Everything breathed for the splendor of the Almighty. So we meet clapping rivers, mountains leaping for joy, stars shouting forth God's splendor. God was not just *like* something, but God *was* a rock, a fortress, a caring shepherd, who brings chaos out of order and hope out of desperation, depending on Israel's fidelity.

*VARIANT
NUMBERING
OF PSALMS–* When the psalms were numbered, the Hebrew and Greek versions divided them differently. What was Psalm 9 in the Greek version, became Psalms 9 and 10 in the Hebrew version. So the numbering of the following psalms is shifted.

For the sake of uniformity, most Bibles today follow the Hebrew numbering. However, some Bibles give both numbers. You can tell whether your Bible is using the Greek or Hebrew numbering by looking at "The Lord is my shepherd," which in the Greek or Catholic version is Psalm 22 and in the Hebrew version is Psalm 23. It might be designated Psalm 23 (22) or Psalm 22 (23).

*The
Responsorial
Psalm in the
Liturgy* Immediately after the first reading, the people are called upon to respond prayerfully to the reading. Ideally, the psalm is chanted by a cantor and the assembly responds in song or prayer. The responsorial psalm, based on the theme of the liturgy, is the people's response to the first reading. It is another way we acknowledge the Lord's presence in the Word.

Just as the psalmist does not focus only on personal concerns but extends his prayer to include the whole human family, so we enlarge our prayer with an awareness and concern for others. This is why the Church incorporates the psalms into our liturgy. In our worship, we are in authentic solidarity with the needs and aspirations of the whole world.

When we empathize with the whole human family, including our Hebrew forebears, the Hebrew Scriptures will be cease to be "old." Instead we will acknowledge

God working anew in our midst through the sacred words proclaimed here and now. The revised liturgy calls us to more active participation in the liturgy. Often we think our cares are the worst, but if we look around, every person is carrying their own share of sorrows and woes. Even if heavy cares burden us, we offer these as prayer. United with the whole Church in an outcry of hope, we are spiritually fortified to bear our burdens.

# PART III

# The New Testament

The part of the Bible unique to Christians, the New Testament, records the life, mission, and teaching of Jesus as well as the tradition that developed among his followers in the first Christian century. It is called "New" because Christians believe Jesus is the fulfillment of the promise of the Messiah foretold in the Hebrew Scriptures. God's love is enfleshed in the person of Jesus.

All Christian churches consider the twenty-seven books of the New Testament, initially written in Greek, as the basis and foundation of the Christian faith. Where the makeup of the New Testament is concerned, there is no difference between Catholic and Protestant, unlike the situation with the Hebrew Scriptures.

However, the New Testament is not really new. It is the continuation of God's Word to believers in a more dramatic way, centering on the person of Jesus, the full revelation of God's love. Remove from the New Testament all Hebrew Scriptural allusions, and it shrinks considerably. Think of the numerous times we read in the New

Testament, "As it is written…" or "As the prophets foretold…." The New Testament was not written in a vacuum but is based on Jesus as the fulfillment of the promises of the Law. Jesus' life, ministry, passion, death, and Resurrection are the hallmark of a Christian's faith. Redemption and eternal happiness are the rewards of a life lived in the spirit of Jesus.

The New Testament—the four Gospels, Acts of the Apostles, Letters, and Revelation (formerly called "the Apocalypse")—spans time from the life of Christ (4 B.C. to A.D. 33) to the second century (A.D. 100). Like the Hebrew Scriptures, the New Testament developed gradually in the faith experience of the Christian community as they proclaimed the Good News of Jesus Christ. Around A.D. 200 the books we now consider the New Testament were acknowledged by all Christians as the scriptural heritage Jesus and the early Church left to us.

**The Four Gospels: Proclamations of the Good News**

The most familiar books of the New Testament are the gospels. These are not biographies but portraits of Jesus as remembered and experienced by his followers. There were many accounts written about Jesus, but only the four gospels were considered to be most truly in keeping with the apostolic message and witness to Jesus.

Why only four gospels? One plausible explanation is that these accounts correspond to the four main centers of Christian activity in which the evangelists ministered. Matthew preached in Jerusalem and Syria among the Jewish Christians. Mark was a disciple of Peter and worked with him in Rome. Luke, a Gentile convert and associate of Paul, ministered to the communities in Asia Minor. John, whose gospel was written in Ephesus at the end of the first century, focused on Jesus' divinity and his relationship with the Father. These four versions of the gospel message proclaimed to specific audiences the life and mission of Jesus.

Although the four gospels are attributed to the evangelists, Matthew, Mark, Luke, and John, they didn't necessarily write the gospels personally. Consider the biblical understanding of authorship. Faith stories developed in the Christian communities and were later committed to writing as the gospels.

Because the first three gospels follow a similar outline of the life of Christ, they are called "synoptic," that is, "seen alongside." They have many parallel passages and seem to share a common source. The Gospel of John emphasizes Jesus' divinity and is written in an altogether different literary genre.

The four gospels provide enough material to show that the Good News of Jesus was truly the fulfillment of the prophetic promises of the Hebrew Scriptures.

*Stages of Development of the Gospels*

The first step in the formation of the gospels was the Christ-event, the time Jesus historically walked this earth. Second, his life and teachings were recalled in the early gatherings after Jesus' death and in the post-Resurrection time by those who actually lived with and rubbed elbows with Jesus.

Imagine how a family gathers after the funeral of a beloved grandmother. They sit around and remember. What do they remember? All that Grandma means for them, how she touched each one.

The early Christian community, so distraught by the absence of Jesus after his death, like a mourning family, gathered to remember. What did they remember? The mystique of the person of Jesus, his life among them.

The gospels as collective memory were possibly

# TIME LINE OF THE
# EARLY CHRISTIAN ERA

| B.C. | | |
|---|---|---|
| ca. 4 | – | Jesus born in Bethlehem |

| A.D. | | |
|---|---|---|
| 30 | – | Jesus lives in Nazareth, called "the hidden life" |
| 30-33 | – | Jesus' ministry and teaching |
| 33 | – | Jesus' passion, death, and Resurrection<br>Pentecost<br>Formation of first Christian community |
| 34 | – | Saul persecutes the Christians |
| 37 | – | Paul converted |
| ca. 40-64 | – | Missionary journeys of Paul |
| 52-64 | – | Epistles of Paul written |
| 63 | – | Persecutions of Christians |
| 64 | – | Peter and Paul martyred in Rome |
| 70-100 | – | Gospels written |
| ca. 120 | – | New Testament completed |
| 200 | – | New Testament approved by early Church |

written backward. The passion, death, and Resurrection were vivid in the disciples' minds and touched them deeply. So these details were given priority when put into writing. That's why all four passion accounts are so similar, although they include different details. Then the disciples recalled the stories and parables Jesus told to get a point across. They also included the miracles of healing. Jesus' discourses developed around collections of sayings and teachings remembered. We have no guarantee that what the gospels record as "Jesus said" actually are the exact words of Jesus.

The infancy narratives, (chapters 1 and 2 of Matthew and Luke) were written last, to show that Jesus truly was human and Jewish and came into this world as all other humans do.

Did the early disciples reach the conclusion that Jesus was the promised Messiah? Did they realize he was God when he was in their midst? Not necessarily. This conviction grew gradually. Let me give a far-fetched yet meaningful analogy. Suppose a foreign royal dignitary's son enrolls anonymously in a college. He attends classes and participates in all activities like any ordinary student. He blends in, and no one realizes his royal roots. At graduation, his identity is revealed. Those who had close contact with him recall instances when his royal demeanor shone through his ordinariness. They remember his allusions to his native land. In hindsight, they come to realize his noble origins.

So also with Jesus. The disciples and close followers knew there was some mystique about him. But they couldn't pinpoint it. There was an aura of mystery about Jesus. At times his followers just couldn't figure him out, but Jesus' whole being exuded goodness and integrity.

After the Resurrection, they remembered and

reminisced. For if Jesus had lived, taught, died, and risen from the dead and no one noticed, what then? There would be no Christianity. Jesus' followers insured that his mission would go on. That is the essence of our Catholic faith: Jesus continues his mission through the Church and our sacramental life.

**MATTHEW**–Matthew's proclamation was addressed to the Jewish followers of Jesus in Jerusalem. It was written around A.D. 85 and is divided, as were the books of Moses, into five distinct sections.

*The Gospels: Purpose and Audience*

**MARK**–Mark's is the shortest gospel and a source of the gospels of Matthew and Luke. It is so believed because most of Mark's gospel is included in Matthew and Luke. Mark was the first gospel, written around A.D. 70 for Gentile Christians in Rome. It considers Jesus, the Son of Man, as a human person with feelings.

**LUKE**–Luke, a Gentile convert to Christianity and a disciple of Paul, writes to Gentile Christians in Asia Minor, who knew little of Jewish culture and background. Luke portrays Jesus as a "man for all. " The universal character of the gospel message is brought out in his choice of material, including women and outcasts of society.

**JOHN**–The Gospel of John, written around A.D. 100, focuses on Jesus' divinity and relationship to the Father. "In the beginning was the Word…and the Word was God" (John 1:1) points directly to the spiritual realm and equates Jesus with God. The episodes chosen have sacramental nuances and are followed by lengthy discourses of a theological nature, regarding the mission of Jesus and the Church.

*History of the Early Church and Saint Paul's Mission*

ACTS OF THE APOSTLES–The Acts of the Apostles, a sequel to the Gospel of Luke and credited to him, is the historical account of the growth of the early Church from Jerusalem to Rome. The first thirteen chapters discuss the early Church in Jerusalem and the ministry of Peter. The ministry and missionary journeys of Paul are recounted in chapters thirteen to twenty-eight and conclude with Paul's imprisonment in Rome. Although the Acts of the Apostles is the most historically accurate of the New Testament accounts, its main purpose is to show how the early Christian community responded to the Good News through the guidance of the Holy Spirit.

*Saint Paul: Apostle to the Gentiles*

We meet Saul, later named Paul, when persecutors laid at his feet the garments of Stephen, the first martyr. A zealous persecutor of the early Christians, Paul was stopped in his tracks by the Lord himself in a dramatic encounter in A.D. 37. Paul came to experience the risen Christ firsthand and became the most dynamic missionary for the cause of Christ. Traveling the Mediterranean countries in three journeys, from Asia Minor to Greece to Rome, Paul established communities of faith wherever he went. He confirmed the people's faith and kept in touch by letters. Since these contained valuable insights in helping Christians understand the faith, the letters were preserved and circulated. Later, when the New Testament was compiled, these letters were considered vital for the spread of Christ's message and the mission of the Church for all time, and so were included in the canon of sacred Scripture. Paul, a faithful follower of the Lord to the end, was martyred in Rome around A.D. 64.

Most of Paul's letters were written to communities of *Letters of* faith to whom he preached the Good News. The earliest *Saint* letter was written around A.D. 52 to the Thessalonians. *Paul* The letters to the Philippians, Philemon, Colossians, and Ephesians are the Captivity Letters because they were written when he was imprisoned. The letters to Timothy and Titus are called "Pastoral Letters," written to individual leaders of churches. Paul incorporated into his being the experience of the risen Christ, Christ who as Redeemer and Savior came to this earth to save all. Paul does not specifically focus on Jesus' ministry while he lived on earth, but Paul considers the risen Christ present in his Mystical Body, the Church. Each letter zeroes in on specific issues or concerns of the local Church as seen through the lens of the thoughts and teachings of Paul. The letters encouraged the young Christian communities to keep the faith.

ROMANS–The Letter to the Romans, the longest and most theologically detailed of Paul's letters, was written around A.D. 57 on Paul's third journey. He addresses the Christian community in Rome, which he had not as yet visited. The necessity of faith for one's salvation figures prominently in the Letter to the Romans, and it contains many points of early Christian doctrine.

FIRST LETTER TO THE CORINTHIANS–Corinth was a thriving commercial center with a diversity of peoples and cultures. Paul addresses the issues of existing factions and morality. The hymn to love, 1 Corinthians 13, is an oft-quoted passage.

**SECOND LETTER TO THE CORINTHIANS**–The Second Letter to the Corinthians is considered a collection of correspondence to the Corinth community. Paul's tone is defensive, attempting to squelch dissensions and attacks on his authority and integrity.

*Captivity Letters*

**GALATIANS**–In his Letter to the Galatians, Paul defends his status as an apostle and warns against agitators who cause dissension. Justification by grace and faith in Jesus, not rituals, or even good works, are signs of a Christian's commitment and freedom in the Spirit.

**EPHESIANS**–The Ephesians are exhorted to live their lives in the Spirit of Christ. The letter expresses Christ's superiority and God's designs in creation and the eternal destiny of those who believe in Christ. There is some doubt as to Paul's authorship of this letter.

**PHILIPPIANS**–The Letter to the Philippians extols joy in suffering for the sake of Christ. Paul encourages the faithful to live in the unselfish spirit of Christ, who abandoned his divinity to become totally immersed in the human condition.

**COLOSSIANS**–The Letter to the Colossians bolsters the faith of the newly-organized community and warns against teachings that rivaled the Christian message.

**PHILEMON**–A touching personal letter of entreaty to Philemon, a wealthy merchant, to take back Onesimus, his slave who had escaped to Rome where he was converted by Paul. Paul asks Philemon to take Onesimus back as a brother in Christ.

**FIRST LETTER TO THE THESSALONIANS**–Thessalonica, an important commercial center, had a large segment of Jewish converts to the faith. They questioned their destiny after death, and Paul reassured them and encouraged fidelity to Christ. Paul speaks of the necessity of being ready for the coming of the Lord.

**SECOND LETTER TO THE THESSALONIANS**–People believed the second coming of Christ was imminent and were worried about life after death. They are encouraged to live life in the Spirit with readiness and watchfulness.

*Pastoral Letters*

Because Timothy and Titus were in charge of churches, the letters addressed to them are called Pastoral Letters. They may have been written by a disciple of Paul.

**FIRST LETTER TO TIMOTHY**–Timothy, a leader of the church in Macedonia, is warned against false teachings and receives advice concerning worship and ministries.

**SECOND LETTER TO TIMOTHY**–This letter contains pastoral directives on how to live the message of Christ faithfully, especially through effective ministry and preaching.

**TITUS**–Titus, a church leader in Crete, is advised how to organize a committed Christian community of faith. This letter outlines the traits of an ideal leader and the danger of false teachings.

*Hebrews*

**HEBREWS**–This letter encourages fellow believers to ward off apostasy and to be faithful to the person of Christ, the High Priest of the New Covenant.

*Catholic*
*(Universal)*
*or Apostolic*
*Letters*

These letters are catholic, not in the sense of Roman Catholic, but catholic in its broad meaning—universal—because they are addressed to a general audience and not a specific community as are the other Letters. Attributed to specific apostles, there is doubt whether each actually wrote them.

**JAMES**–The Letter of James, written by a leader of the Church around A.D. 90, exhorts believers to put their faith into action and to fight against the evils of the day by pious upright lives in accordance with the Good News. The most noted passage is James 5:14-16, which recommends calling in the presbyters for healing when one is sick. It is used as a scriptural reference to the sacrament of the sick.

**FIRST LETTER OF PETER**–The author stresses the dignity of the Christian vocation and exhorts readers to be firm in the faith despite persecution.

**SECOND LETTER OF PETER**–Written for converts from Jewish and Greek culture, it is similar to the Letter of Jude. It upholds belief in God's judgment and the Second Coming of Christ.

**FIRST LETTER OF JOHN**–The three Johannine Letters appeal to Christians of the churches to be faithful to their tradition. God is love, and so Christians, too, must be marked by their love.

**SECOND LETTER OF JOHN**–This letter is addressed to Christians, encouraging them to love and to be steadfast in their faith in Jesus, so as to counteract the heretics who denied the reality of the Incarnation.

**THIRD LETTER OF JOHN**–A letter to Gaius, a wealthy Christian, the author commends his hospitality and aid to missionaries as true Christian virtue.

**JUDE**–This short letter, written around A.D. 90 by Jude, a leader of the Jerusalem church, warns against conflicting teachings of various communities at the time.

*Revelation: New Testament Prophetic Book*

A vision of final triumph for the persecuted early Church, the Book of Revelation is the least understood book of the Bible. Although it is classed as prophetic, it does not foretell specific future events. The author, using cryptic language and symbolism, shows that good and evil co-exist, but that, in the end, good and the reign of God will prevail. This language and symbolism was easily understood by those early Christians to whom it was addressed. To understand its message today, the reader needs to see not a foreboding of the end of the world but an expression of the perennial struggle between good and evil and a celebration of the ultimate victory of good. To do this, the reader accepts the language of Revelation as symbolic, as did the early Christians.

# PART IV

# Making the Bible Part of Our Spirituality and Prayer

The renewal of Vatican II encouraged a deeper understanding of the Scriptures by emphasizing the Word as an integral part of our worship. It also encouraged Catholics to make greater use of the Bible through devotional reading and prayer. The Bible, unlike any other book that we can put aside or ignore, is a prototype of how God acts in the lives of all people, including you in your present situation.

Since Catholics have not been accustomed to pick up the Bible for private devotion and prayer, here are some practical ways to profit from using the Bible for personal spiritual growth. The purpose in using the Bible in your personal prayer is to assist you to relate to God better and grow in your closeness to God. Private prayer is for ourselves, but it is also a good crop that can be tilled back into our liturgy, enriching it for ourselves and for the whole community. Before opening the Bible, pray for divine guidance, that through the sacred words you may hear the Lord speak to you in your present situation for your own good and the good of all concerned.

Although we may know the story of biblical times, we often remain focused on the historical facts and fail to apply Scripture to our lives. It is easier to know a subject than to live it. The best and easiest way to make Scripture part of our faith life is to approach the Scriptures in faith and with feeling.

Choose a Bible with which you feel comfortable. The Bible is available in a variety of versions and formats. Large volumes may contain detailed footnotes, explanatory notes, and cross references. Smaller versions are convenient to carry with you. It doesn't matter what version you choose. Select one that is user-friendly, one in which you feel free to underline, highlight, or make notations that help in your prayer.

After you select your Bible, where do you begin? Don't be a marathon Bible-reader, reading it from cover to cover in record time. The selection you choose can be from the liturgical readings or it may be another passage to which you are drawn. There are parts of the Bible that are easier to relate to and understand than others. Consult the table of contents in front of your Bible to help you select a passage, and prayerfully ask to be guided in your choice.

Your selection also depends on the purpose you have in mind.

*For information.* Sometimes you may want to read the Bible just to familiarize yourself with it.

*For spiritual uplift.* The words of comfort of the prophets, psalms, or Jesus may be your solace in times of difficulty, depression, or heartache.

*For prayer.* You can use Scripture as a prayer book. Because we know not how to pray as we ought, the Bible puts into our souls the Spirit of God and enables us to speak to God in God's own words.

*To prepare to hear the Word of God at Mass.* Reading and praying the lectionary readings as personal prayer has a dual effect: it brings us personally closer to God, and, when we then celebrate with the community at Mass, God uses us to enrich the whole community in ways that we might not even imagine. But we can rest assured that our increased prayerfulness is a blessing both to ourselves and to others. Beginning on page 70 is an appendix listing all the Sunday readings for all the cycles. You can use it anytime to prepare for Sunday Mass.

After you select a passage, read it prayerfully and slowly. Reflect on its meaning, using the following questions. Is it saying anything to me of my relationship with God? What is the message God's Word has for me? Why is this a part of the Bible? What does it say about the relationship between God and me? What is my attitude at this moment? What does it relay to me of God's working in my life?

Take a few moments to talk it over with God in reflective and conversational prayer.

Pause and reflect. Listen also. Praying doesn't necessarily have to be expressed in words. It can be simply placing ourselves in God's presence. Listening to the Word is as important as reading and hearing the Word.

When God speaks, we need to listen. Maybe a new insight will come to mind. If one passage hits you, stay with it. Savor it. Talk it over with the Lord. Reflect on its meaning for you. Determine how this passage can help you be a better person.

Cultivate the habit of daily Bible reading. Set aside a certain time in your daily routine. Like other resolutions, Bible reading needs to be nurtured and practiced as a good habit. But once you delve into Scripture, the spiritual enrichment you taste will whet your appetite for more.

*Praying with the Hebrew Scriptures*

A logical place to start to pray the Hebrew Scriptures is the Book of Psalms. As explained at the end of Part Two, the psalms are prayers of the human heart for all occasions.

*Practical Pointers for Reading the Gospels*

Each gospel gives a specific portrait of the person of Jesus. Consider the audience and purpose of a particular gospel. Do not expect a full-blown biography of Jesus. Instead, understand that each gospel presents a carefully selected sequence of events according to the gospel writer's theological purpose.

The gospels are not strictly historical accounts, but a theological history, told to convey a spiritual truth about Jesus and his teachings. Do not take the accounts as literally accurate. Otherwise, the conflicting details in the gospels will seem confusing. Keep in mind that the gospels are a written result of what was handed on about Jesus. They were not intended as blow-by-blow descriptions of Jesus' life and mission.

When hearing the gospel read at the Sunday liturgy, we hear just a snippet or portion, one episode, miracle story, or parable. To profit more from the gospels, why not read an entire gospel in one sitting? You get a feel for the individual flavor of each evangelist's style and purpose. Then you can better see the individual portrait of Jesus each evangelist presents. As you read each gospel, allow the Jesus of that particular evangelist to emerge.

As you peruse Matthew, notice how the book is divided into five sections, like the Torah. The Law of Moses is surpassed by the Good News that Jesus proclaims. The Sermon on the Mount in chapters 5-7 is reminiscent of Moses on Mount Sinai. Jesus as the new Moses proclaims the Good News. The Sermon takes place on a mountain as did Moses' receiving the Ten Commandments. Matthew wrote for Jews, and so he alludes to Jewish customs and the fact that Jesus fulfilled the promises of the Old Covenant, "as it was written...."

Mark, the shortest and earliest gospel, gives us a glimpse of a human Jesus. Tradition has it that Mark, a companion of Peter, witnessed the persecutions of A.D. 64. To preserve the memories of Peter for future generations, Mark wrote the gospel. In Mark, Jesus is an active Jesus, always doing, a man who never rests. You feel you are on fast forward. Mark doesn't bother with long discourses or descriptions, but shows Jesus on the move. In the Gospel of Mark, Jesus is the human Jesus, with all human emotions.

The third gospel, Luke, along with Matthew, includes most of the Marcan material. Luke, as a Gentile writing for the Gentile Christians, portrays Jesus as compassionate and sympathetic. Notice how women and the downtrodden feature prominently in Luke. Only in Luke do we hear of the Prodigal Son, Good Samaritan, and Mary and Martha. Luke takes you on a journey from Galilee to Jerusalem where Jesus met his death. Luke's account continues in the Acts of the Apostles.

As you read John's Gospel, be prepared to enter a transcendent world. This is not the Jesus who trod the roads of Palestine but a Jesus whose origin is from the beginning in God: "The Word was God" (John 1:1). John wrote his gospel decades after the other gospels, and so John depicts a Jesus who is not only human but also totally divine. The episodes of Nicodemus, the marriage at Cana, the feeding of the multitude, and the promise of the Spirit prefigure the sacramental life of the Church.

*Reading the Letters*

Of all the Scripture readings, the section you can most readily apply to your life are the letters. These letters of Paul and other apostles contain practical advice in living out your Christian commitment. To understand the cultural nuances, it is advisable to read in your Bible the purpose and introduction to each, to get a background of the circumstances the letter addresses. This advice is pertinent to all the books of the Bible.

*The Book of Revelation*

This seemingly difficult book of the Bible contains a simple message. Beneath the esoteric symbols and colorful imagery is the promise of hope. The Book of Revelation does not purport to be a foreboding of events to come. It addresses the mystery of God's justice and love. Although good and evil exist in this world, ultimately good will prevail. This is the hope and promise of the Book of Revelation.

This book cannot be taken literally, for it originally intended to convey a symbolic message of hope to Christians who were being persecuted. When you are confronted by someone who interprets the passages as prophecy, rather than arguing, simply state, "To me God seems to be saying...." This attitude forestalls unnecessary theological squabbles.

# Conclusion

The Bible, the Word of God, speaks loudly to those who hear. It is much more than a static record of past events but is a meaningful instrument to strengthen our relationship with God and help us learn how God acts in our lives today. If we allow the Lord so to break into our lives, Scripture fulfills its noble role. Allow the Lord to challenge, speak, and work spiritual marvels in your life, both in the hearing of the Word during the liturgy and in your private devotional moments.

# Appendix

# The Lectionary and the Liturgical Year

Through its rich liturgical obvservances, the Church remembers and keeps alive the message and mission of Jesus around the flow of the various natural seasons. The liturgical cycles, with their plethora of feasts and holy days, help us appropriate the mystery of Christ into our ordinary lives. We all have our new beginnings, our rebirths, our sufferings, dyings, resurrections, and glories. We incorporate the mystery of Christ by awareness of the significance of the liturgical calendar.

The beginning of the liturgical year is the season of Advent. The Christmas cycle recalls great joy in Christ's birth and lasts until the Baptism of the Lord, which is the first part of Ordinary Time. The Lenten, Easter, and Pentecost seasons follow. The in-between time—Ordinary Time—lasts from around the end of June until Advent. The number of Sundays in Ordinary Time varies from year to year depending on the date of Easter. This table lists the readings for Ordinary Time after the Easter cycle (Trinity Sunday).

The revised liturgy has designated Sunday readings in three-year cycles (Cycles A, B, and C), so the laity may be exposed to more scriptural passages. The following table is a quick reference to the readings for the Sundays and holy days of the liturgical year. The abbreviations are those of the *New American Bible*.

# The Sunday Readings

| CYCLE A | CYCLE B | CYCLE C |
|---------|---------|---------|

### -First Sunday of Advent-

| | | |
|---|---|---|
| Is. 2:1-5 | Is. 63:16-19; 64:2-7 | Jer. 33:14-16 |
| Ps. 122:1-9 | Ps. 80:2-19 | Ps. 25:4-14 |
| Rom. 13:11-14 | 1 Cor. 1:3-9 | 1 Thes. 3:12—4:2 |
| Mt. 24:37-44 | Mk. 13:33-37 | Lk. 21:25-28,34-36 |

### -Second Sunday of Advent-

| | | |
|---|---|---|
| Is. 11:1-10 | Is. 40:1-5, 9-11 | Bar. 5:1-9 |
| Ps. 72:1-17 | Ps. 85:9-14 | Ps. 126:1–6 |
| Rom. 15:4-9 | 2 Pt. 3:8-14 | Phil. 1:4-11 |
| Mt. 3:1-12 | Mk. 1:1-8 | Lk. 3:1-6 |

### -Third Sunday of Advent-

| | | |
|---|---|---|
| Is. 35:1-6,10 | Is. 61:1- 2,10-11 | Zep. 3:14-18 |
| Ps. 146:6-10 | Lk. 1:46-54 | Is. 12:2-6 |
| Jas. 5:7-10 | 1 Thes. 5:16-24 | Phil. 4:4-7 |
| Mt. 11:2-11 | Jn. 1:6-8; 19-28 | Lk. 3:10-18 |

### -Fourth Sunday of Advent-

| | | |
|---|---|---|
| Is. 7:10-14 | 2 Sm. 7:1-16 | Mi. 5:1-4 |
| Ps. 24:1-6 | Ps. 89:2-5,27-29 | Ps. 80:2-3,15-19 |
| Rom. 1:1-7 | Rom. 16:25-27 | Heb. 10:5-10 |
| Mt. 1:18-24 | Lk. 1:26-38 | Lk. 1:39-45 |

### -Solemnity of Christmas-

| **Midnight Mass** | **Mass at Dawn** | **Mass During the Day** |
|---|---|---|
| Is. 9:1-6 | Is. 62:11-12 | Is. 52:7-10 |
| Ps. 96:1-3,11-13 | Ps. 97:1,6,11-12 | Ps. 98:1-6 |
| Ti. 2:11-14 | Ti. 3:4-7 | Heb. 1:1-6 |
| Lk. 2:1-14 | Lk. 2:15-20 | Jn. 1:1-18 |

| CYCLE A | CYCLE B | CYCLE C |
|---------|---------|---------|

## -Sunday within Octave of Christmas—Holy Family-

| CYCLE A | CYCLE B | CYCLE C |
|---------|---------|---------|
| Sir. 3:2-7,12-14 | Sir. 3:2-7,12-14 | Sir. 3:2-7,12-14 |
| Ps. 128:1-5 | Ps. 128:1-5 | Ps. 128:1-5 |
| Col. 3:12-21 | Col. 3:12-21 | Col. 3:12-21 |
| Mt. 2:13-15,19-23 | Lk. 2:22-40 | Lk. 2:41-52 |

## -Solemnity of Mary, Mother of God-

Nm. 6:22-27    (Readings the same in all cycles)
Ps. 67:2-8
Gal. 4:4-7
Lk. 2:16-21

## -Solemnity of the Epiphany-
### *(Three Kings)*

Is. 60:1-6     (Readings the same in all cycles)
Ps. 72:1-13
Eph. 3:2-6
Mt. 2:1-12

## -Sunday after Epiphany—Baptism of the Lord-
### *(First Sunday of Ordinary Time)*

| CYCLE A | CYCLE B | CYCLE C |
|---------|---------|---------|
| Is. 42:1-7 | Is. 42:1-7 | Is. 42:1-7 |
| Ps. 29:1-10 | Ps. 29:1-10 | Ps. 29:1-10 |
| Acts 10:34-38 | Acts 10:34-38 | Acts 10:34-38 |
| Mt. 3:13-17 | Mk. 1:7-11 | Lk. 3:15-22 |

## -First Sunday of Lent-

| CYCLE A | CYCLE B | CYCLE C |
|---------|---------|---------|
| Gn. 2:7-9; 3:1-7 | Gn. 9:8-15 | Dt. 26:4-10 |
| Ps. 51:3-17 | Ps. 25:4-9 | Ps. 91:1-15 |
| Rom. 5:12-19 | 1 Pt. 3:18-22 | Rom. 10:8-13 |
| Mt. 4:1-11 | Mk. 1:12-15 | Lk. 4:1-13 |

| CYCLE A | CYCLE B | CYCLE C |
|---------|---------|---------|

### -Second Sunday of Lent-

| | | |
|---------|---------|---------|
| Gn. 12:1-4 | Gn. 22:1-18 | Gn. 15:5-12,17-18 |
| Ps. 33:4,5,18-22 | Ps. 116:10-19 | Ps. 27:1-14 |
| 2 Tm. 1:8-10 | Rom. 8:31-34 | Phil. 3:17—4:1 |
| Mt. 17:1-9 | Mk. 9:2-10 | Lk. 9:28-36 |

### -Third Sunday of Lent-

| | | |
|---------|---------|---------|
| Ex. 17:3-7 | Ex. 20: 1-17 | Ex. 3:1-8,13-15 |
| Ps. 95:1-9 | Ps. 19:8-11 | Ps. 103:1-11 |
| Rom. 5:1-8 | 1 Cor. 1:22-25 | 1 Cor. 10:1-6,10-12 |
| Jn. 4:5-42 | Jn 2:13-25 | Lk. 13:1-9 |
| | or Cycle A readings | or Cycle A readings |

### -Fourth Sunday of Lent-

| | | |
|---------|---------|---------|
| 1 Sm. 16:1,6-13 | 2 Chr. 36:14-23 | Jos. 5:9-12 |
| Ps. 23:1-6 | Ps. 137:1-6 | Ps. 34:2-7 |
| Eph. 5:8-14 | Eph. 2:4-10 | 2 Cor. 5:17-21 |
| John 9:1-41 | John 3:14-21 | Lk. 15:1-3,11-32 |
| | or Cycle A readings | or Cycle A readings |

### -Fifth Sunday of Lent-

| | | |
|---------|---------|---------|
| Ez. 37:12-14 | Jer. 31:31-34 | Is. 43:16-21 |
| Ps. 130:1-8 | Ps. 51:3-15 | Ps. 126:1-6 |
| Rom. 8:8-11 | Heb. 5:7-9 | Phil. 3:8-14 |
| Jn. 11:1-45 | Jn. 12:20-33 | Jn. 8:1-11 |
| | or Cycle A readings | or Cycle A readings |

### -Passion (Palm) Sunday-

| | | |
|---------|---------|---------|
| Is. 50:4-7 | Is. 50:4-7 | Is. 50:4-7 |
| Ps. 22:8-24 | Ps. 22:8-24 | Ps. 22:8-24 |
| Phil. 2:6-11 | Phil. 2:6-11 | Phil. 2:6-11 |
| Mt. 26:14—27:66 | Mk. 14:1-15 | Lk. 22:14—23:56 |
| or 27:11-54 | or 15:1-39 | or 23:1-49 |

| CYCLE A | CYCLE B | CYCLE C |
|---------|---------|---------|

## -Solemnity of Easter-

Acts 10:34-43        (Readings the same in all cycles)
Ps. 118:1-23
Col. 3:1-4
Jn. 20:1-9

The Solemnity of Easter Vigil begins Easter time. The Thursday after the Sixth Sunday of Easter is Ascension Thursday. (In some dioceses, this has been moved to the Seventh Sunday of Easter.) Ten days later (the Eighth Sunday) is the Solemnity of Pentecost, which is followed by Trinity Sunday, the end of the Easter season. In places where the Solemnity of the Body and Blood of Christ is not a holy day, as in the USA, it is observed on the Ninth Sunday after Easter. Ordinary Time is observed until the first Sunday of Advent, when the new liturgical cycle begins.

## -Second Sunday of Easter-

| Acts 2:42-47 | Acts 4:32-35 | Acts 5:12-16 |
|--------------|--------------|--------------|
| Ps. 118:2-24 | Ps. 118:2-24 | Ps. 118:2-24 |
| 1 Pt. 1:3-9 | 1 Jn. 5:1-6 | Rev. 1:9-19 |
| Jn. 20:19-31 | Jn. 20:19-31 | Jn. 20:19-31 |

## -Third Sunday of Easter-

| Acts: 2:14-28 | Acts 3:13-19 | Acts 5:27-41 |
|---------------|--------------|--------------|
| Ps. 16:1-16 | Ps. 4:2-9 | Ps. 30:2-13 |
| 1 Pt. 1:17-21 | 1 Jn. 2:1-5 | Rv. 5:11-14 |
| Lk. 24:13-35 | Lk. 24:35-48 | Jn. 21:1-19 |

## -Fourth Sunday of Easter-

| Acts 2:14,36-41 | Acts 4:8-12 | Acts 13:14,43-52 |
|-----------------|-------------|------------------|
| Ps. 23:1-6 | Ps. 118:8-29 | Ps. 100:1-5 |
| 1 Pt. 2:20-25 | 1 Jn. 3:1-2 | Rv. 7:9,14-17 |
| Jn. 10:1-10 | Jn.10 :11-18 | Jn. 10:27-30 |

| CYCLE A | CYCLE B | CYCLE C |
| --- | --- | --- |

## -Fifth Sunday of Easter-

| | | |
| --- | --- | --- |
| Acts 6:1-7 | Acts 9:26-31 | Acts 14:21-27 |
| Ps. 33:1-5,18-19 | Ps. 22:26-32 | Ps. 145:8-13 |
| 1 Pt. 2:4-9 | 1 Jn. 3:18-24 | Rv. 21:1-5 |
| Jn. 14:1-12 | Jn. 15:1-8 | Jn. 13:31-35 |

## -Sixth Sunday of Easter-

| | | |
| --- | --- | --- |
| Acts 8:5-17 | Acts 10:25-48 | Acts 15:1-2,22-29 |
| Ps. 66:1-20 | Ps. 98:1-4 | Ps. 67:2-8 |
| 1 Pt. 3:15-18 | 1 Jn. 4:7-10 | Rv. 21:10-23 |
| Jn. 14:15-21 | Jn. 15:9-17 | Jn. 14:23-29 |

## -Solemnity of the Ascension -

| | | |
| --- | --- | --- |
| Acts 1:1-11 | Acts 1:1-11 | Acts 1:1-11 |
| Ps. 47:2-9 | Ps. 47:2-9 | Ps. 47:2-9 |
| Eph. 1:17-23 | Eph. 1:17-23 | Eph. 1:17-23 |
| Mt. 28:16-20 | Mk. 16:15-20 | Lk. 24:46-53 |

## -Seventh Sunday of Easter-
### (Solemnity of the Ascension in some dioceses)

| | | |
| --- | --- | --- |
| Acts 1:12-14 | Acts 1:15-26 | Acts 7:55-60 |
| Ps. 27:1-8 | Ps. 103:1-2,11-20 | Ps. 97:1-9 |
| 1 Pt. 4:13-16 | 1 Jn. 4:11-16 | Rv. 22:12-20 |
| Jn. 17:1-11 | Jn. 17:11-19 | Jn. 17:20-26 |

## -Solemnity of Pentecost-

| | |
| --- | --- |
| Acts 2:1-11 | (Readings are the same in all cycles) |
| Ps. 104:24-34 | |
| 1 Cor. 12:3-13 | |
| Jn. 20:19-23 | |

## -Solemnity of Trinity Sunday-

| | | |
| --- | --- | --- |
| Ex. 34:4-9 | Dt. 4:32-40 | Prv. 8:22-31 |
| Dn. 3:52-56 | Ps. 33:4-9,18-22 | Ps. 8:4-9 |
| 2 Cor. 13:11-13 | Rom. 8:14-17 | Rom. 5:1-5 |
| Jn. 3:16-18 | Mt. 28:16-20 | Jn. 16:12-15 |

| CYCLE A | CYCLE B | CYCLE C |
| --- | --- | --- |

## -Solemnity of the Body and Blood of Christ-

| | | |
| --- | --- | --- |
| Dt. 8:2-3,14-16 | Ex. 24:3-8 | Gn. 14:18-20 |
| Ps. 147:12-20 | Ps. 116:12-18 | Ps. 110:1-4 |
| 1 Cor. 10:16-17 | Heb. 9:11-15 | 1 Cor. 11:23-26 |
| Jn. 6:51-58 | Mk. 14:12-14, 22-26 | Lk. 9:11-17 |

## -Second Sunday in Ordinary Time-

| | | |
| --- | --- | --- |
| Is. 49:3-6 | 1 Sm. 3:3-19 | Is. 62:1-5 |
| Ps. 40:2-10 | Ps. 40:2-10 | Ps. 96:1-10 |
| 1 Cor. 1:1-3 | 1 Cor. 6:13-20 | 1 Cor. 12:4-11 |
| Jn. 1:29-34 | Jn. 1:35-42 | Jn. 2:1-11 |

## -Third Sunday in Ordinary Time-

| | | |
| --- | --- | --- |
| Is. 8:23—9:3 | Jon. 3:1-10 | Neh. 8:2-10 |
| Ps. 27:1-14 | Ps. 25:4-9 | Ps. 19:8-15 |
| 1 Cor. 1:10-17 | 1 Cor. 7:29-31 | 1 Cor. 12:12-30 |
| Mt. 4:12-23 | Mk. 1:14-20 | Lk. 1:1-4; 4:14-21 |

## -Fourth Sunday in Ordinary Time-

| | | |
| --- | --- | --- |
| Zep. 2:3; 3:12-13 | Dt. 18:15-20 | Jer. 1:4-19 |
| Ps. 146:6-10 | Ps. 95:1-9 | Ps. 71:1-17 |
| 1 Cor. 1:26-31 | 1 Cor. 7:32-35 | 1 Cor. 12:31—13:31 |
| Mt. 5:1-12 | Mk. 1:21-28 | Lk. 4:21-30 |

## -Fifth Sunday in Ordinary Time-

| | | |
| --- | --- | --- |
| Is. 58:7-10 | Jb. 7:1-7 | Is. 6:1-8 |
| Ps. 112:4-9 | Ps. 147:1-6 | Ps. 138:1-8 |
| 1 Cor. 2:1-5 | 1 Cor. 9:16-23 | 1 Cor. 15:1-11 |
| Mt 5:13-16 | Mk 1:29-39 | Lk. 5:1-11 |

## -Sixth Sunday in Ordinary Time-

| | | |
| --- | --- | --- |
| Sir. 15:15-20 | Lv. 13:1-2,42-46 | Jer. 17:5-8 |
| Ps. 119:1-34 | Ps. 32:1-11 | Ps. 1:1-6 |
| 1 Cor. 2:6-10 | 1 Cor. 10:31—11:1 | 1 Cor. 15:12,16-20 |
| Mt. 5:17-37 | Mk. 1:40-45 | Lk. 6:17-26 |

| CYCLE A | CYCLE B | CYCLE C |
|---------|---------|---------|

### -Seventh Sunday in Ordinary Time-

| Lv. 19:1-2,17-18 | Is. 43:18-25 | 1 Sm. 26:2,7-23 |
|---------|---------|---------|
| Ps. 103:1-13 | Ps. 41:2-14 | Ps. 103:1-13 |
| 1 Cor. 3:16-23 | 2 Cor. 1:18-22 | 1 Cor. 15:45–49 |
| Mt. 5:38-48 | Mk. 2:1-12 | Lk. 6:27-38 |

### -Eighth Sunday in Ordinary Time-

| Is. 49:14-15 | Hos. 2 :16-22 | Sir. 27:4-7 |
|---------|---------|---------|
| Ps. 62:2-9 | Ps. 103:1-13 | Ps. 92:2-16 |
| 1 Cor. 4:1-5 | 2 Cor. 3:1-6 | 1 Cor. 15:54-58 |
| Mt. 6:24-34 | Mk. 2:18-22 | Lk. 6:39-45 |

### -Ninth Sunday in Ordinary Time-

| Dt. 11:18,26-28,32 | Dt. 5:12-151 | 1 Kings 8:41-43 |
|---------|---------|---------|
| Ps. 31:2-25 | Ps. 81:3-11 | Ps. 117:1,2 |
| Rom. 3:21-28 | 2 Cor. 4:6-11 | Gal. 1:1-10 |
| Mt. 7:21-27 | Mk.. 2:23-28 | Lk. 7:1-10 |

### -Tenth Sunday in Ordinary Time-

| Hos. 6:3-6 | Gn. 3:9-15 | 1 Kgs. 17:17-24 |
|---------|---------|---------|
| Ps. 50:1-15 | Ps. 130:1-8 | Ps. 30:2-13 |
| Rom. 4:18-25 | 2 Cor. 4:13—5:1 | Gal. 1:11-19 |
| Mt. 9:9-13 | Mk. 3:20-35 | Lk. 7:11-17 |

### -Eleventh Sunday in Ordinary Time-

| Ex. 19:2-6 | Ez. 17:22-24 | 2 Sm. 12:7-13 |
|---------|---------|---------|
| Ps. 100:1-5 | Ps. 92:2-16 | Ps. 32:1-11 |
| Rom. 5:6-11 | 2 Cor. 5:6-10 | Gal. 2:16-21 |
| Mt. 9:36—10:8 | Mk. 4:26-34 | Lk. 7:36-50 |

### -Twelfth Sunday in Ordinary Time-

| Jer. 20:10-13 | Jb. 38:1,8-11 | Zec. 12:10-11; 13:1 |
|---------|---------|---------|
| Ps. 69:8-17,33-35 | Ps. 107:23-31 | Ps. 63:2-9 |
| Rom. 5:12-15 | 2 Cor. 5:14-17 | Gal. 3:26-29 |
| Mt. 10:26-33 | Mk. 4:35-41 | Lk. 9:18-24 |

| CYCLE A | CYCLE B | CYCLE C |
|---------|---------|---------|

### -Thirteenth Sunday in Ordinary Time-

| | | |
|---------|---------|---------|
| 2 Kgs. 4:8-16 | Wis. 1:13-15; 2:23-24 | 1 Kgs. 19:16-21 |
| Ps. 89:2-3,16-19 | Ps. 30:2-13 | Ps. 16:1-11 |
| Rom. 6:3-11 | 2 Cor. 8:7-15 | Gal. 5:1,13-18 |
| Mt. 10:37-42 | Mk. 5:21-43 | Lk. 9:51-62 |

### -Fourteenth Sunday in Ordinary Time-

| | | |
|---------|---------|---------|
| Zec. 9:9,10 | Ez. 2:2-5 | Is. 66:10-14 |
| Ps. 145:1-14 | Ps. 123:1-4 | Ps. 66:1-20 |
| Rom. 8:9-13 | 2 Cor. 12:7-10 | Gal. 6:14-18 |
| Mt. 11:25-30 | Mk. 6:1-6 | Lk. 10:1-20 |

### -Fifteenth Sunday in Ordinary Time-

| | | |
|---------|---------|---------|
| Is. 55:10-11 | Am. 7:12-15 | Dt. 30:10-14 |
| Ps. 65:10-14 | Ps. 85:9-14 | Ps. 69:14,17,30-37 |
| Rom. 8:18-23 | Eph. 1:3-14 | Col. 1:15-20 |
| Mt. 13:1-23 | Mk. 6:7-13 | Lk. 10:25-37 |

### -Sixteenth Sunday in Ordinary Time-

| | | |
|---------|---------|---------|
| Wis. 12:13-19 | Jer. 23:1-6 | Gn. 18:1-10 |
| Ps. 86:5-16 | Ps. 23:1-6 | Ps. 15:2-5 |
| Rom. 8:26-27 | Eph. 2:13-18 | Col. 1:24-28 |
| Mt. 13:24-43 | Mk. 6:30-34 | Lk. 10:38-42 |

### -Seventeenth Sunday in Ordinary Time-

| | | |
|---------|---------|---------|
| 1 Kgs. 3:5-12 | 2 Kgs. 4:42-44 | Gn. 18:20-32 |
| Ps. 119:127-130 | Ps. 145:10-18 | Ps. 138:1-8 |
| Rom. 8:28-30 | Eph. 4:1-6 | Col. 2:12-14 |
| Mt. 13:44-52 | Jn. 6:1-15 | Lk. 11:1-13 |

### -Eighteenth Sunday in Ordinary Time-

| | | |
|---------|---------|---------|
| Is. 55:1-3 | Ex.16:2-4,12-15 | Eccl. 1:2; 2:21-23 |
| Ps. 145:8-18 | Ps. 78:3,4,23-25 | Ps. 90:3-17 |
| Rom. 8:35-39 | Eph. 4:17-24 | Col. 3:1-11 |
| Mt. 14:13-21 | Jn. 6:24-35 | Lk. 12:13-21 |

| CYCLE A | CYCLE B | CYCLE C |
|---------|---------|---------|

### -Nineteenth Sunday in Ordinary Time-

| | | |
|---------|---------|---------|
| 1 Kgs. 19:9-13 | 1 Kgs. 19:4-8 | Wis. 18:6-9 |
| Ps. 85:9-14 | Ps. 34:2-9 | Ps. 33:18-22 |
| Rom. 9:1-5 | Eph. 4:30—5:2 | Heb. 11:1-2,8-19 |
| Mt. 14:22-33 | Jn. 6:41-51 | Lk. 12:32- 48 |

### -Twentieth Sunday in Ordinary Time-

| | | |
|---------|---------|---------|
| Is. 56:1-7 | Prv. 9:1-6 | Jer. 38:4-10 |
| Ps. 67:2-8 | Ps. 34:2-17 | Ps. 40:2-18 |
| Rom. 11:13-32 | Eph. 5:15-20 | Heb. 12:1-4 |
| Mt. 15:21-28 | Jn. 6:51-58 | Lk. 12:49-53 |

### -Twenty-first Sunday in Ordinary Time-

| | | |
|---------|---------|---------|
| Is. 22:19-23 | Jos. 24:1-18 | Is. 66:18-21 |
| Ps. 138:1-8 | Ps. 34:2-21 | Ps. 117:1-2 |
| Rom. 11:33-36 | Eph. 5:21-32 | Heb. 12:5-13 |
| Mt. 16:13-20 | Jn. 6:60- 69 | Lk. 13:22-30 |

### -Twenty-second Sunday in Ordinary Time-

| | | |
|---------|---------|---------|
| Jer. 20:7-9 | Dt. 4:1-8 | Sir. 3:17-18,20, 28-29 |
| Ps. 63:2-9 | Ps. 15:2-5 | Ps. 68:4-11 |
| Rom. 12:1,2 | Jas. 1:17-27 | Heb. 12:18-24 |
| Mt. 16:21-27 | Mk. 7:1-8,14-15, 21-23 | Lk. 14:1,7-14 |

### -Twenty-third Sunday in Ordinary Time-

| | | |
|---------|---------|---------|
| Ez. 33:7-9 | Is. 35:4-7 | Wis. 9:13-18 |
| Ps. 95:1-9 | Ps. 146:7-10 | Ps. 90:3-17 |
| Rom. 13:8-10 | Jas. 2:1-5 | Phlm. 9-10,12-17 |
| Mt. 18:15-20 | Mk. 7:31-37 | Lk. 14:25-33 |

| CYCLE A | CYCLE B | CYCLE C |
| --- | --- | --- |

### -Twenty-fourth Sunday in Ordinary Time-

| | | |
| --- | --- | --- |
| Sir. 27:30—28:9 | Is. 50:5-9 | Ex. 32:7-14 |
| Ps. 103:1-12 | Ps. 116:1-9 | Ps. 51:3-19 |
| Rom. 14:7-9 | Jas. 2:14-18 | 1 Tm. 1:12-17 |
| Mt. 18:21-35 | Mk. 8:27-35 | Lk. 15:1-32 |

### -Twenty-fifth Sunday in Ordinary Time-

| | | |
| --- | --- | --- |
| Is. 55:6-9 | Wis. 2:12,17-20 | Am. 8:4-7 |
| Ps. 145:2-18 | Ps. 54:3-8 | Ps. 113:1-8 |
| Phil. 1:20-27 | Jas. 3:16—4:3 | 1 Tm. 2:1-8 |
| Mt. 20:1-16 | Mk. 9:30-37 | Lk. 16:1-13 |

### -Twenty-sixth Sunday in Ordinary Time-

| | | |
| --- | --- | --- |
| Ez. 18:25-28 | Nm. 11:25-29 | Am. 6:4-7 |
| Ps. 25:4-9 | Ps. 19:8-14 | Ps. 146:7-10 |
| Phil. 2:1-11 | Jas. 5:1-6 | 1 Tm. 6:11-16 |
| Mt. 21:28-32 | Mk. 9:38- 48 | Lk. 16:19-31 |

### -Twenty-seventh Sunday in Ordinary Time-

| | | |
| --- | --- | --- |
| Is. 5:1-7 | Gn. 2:18-24 | Hab. 1:2-3; 2:2-4 |
| Ps. 80:9-20 | Ps. 128:1-6 | Ps. 95:1-9 |
| Phil. 4:6-9 | Heb. 2:9-11 | 2 Tm. 1:6-14 |
| Mt. 21:33-43 | Mk. 10:2-16 | Lk. 17:5-10 |

### -Twenty-eighth Sunday in Ordinary Time-

| | | |
| --- | --- | --- |
| Is. 25:6-10 | Wis. 7:7-11 | 2 Kgs. 5:14-17 |
| Ps. 23:1-6 | Ps. 90:12-17 | Ps. 98:1-4 |
| Phil. 4:12-20 | Heb. 4:12-13 | 2 Tm. 2:8-13 |
| Mt. 22:1-14 | Mk. 10:17-30 | Lk. 17:11-19 |

### -Twenty-ninth Sunday in Ordinary Time-

| | | |
| --- | --- | --- |
| Is. 45:1-6 | Is. 53:10-11 | Ex. 17:8-13 |
| Ps. 96:1-10 | Ps. 33:4-5,18-22 | Ps. 121:1-8 |
| 1 Thes.1:1-5 | Heb. 4:14-16 | 2 Tm. 3:14—4:2 |
| Mt. 22:15-21 | Mk. 10:35-45 | Lk. 18:1-8 |

| CYCLE A | CYCLE B | CYCLE C |
|---------|---------|---------|

### -Thirtieth Sunday in Ordinary Time-

| CYCLE A | CYCLE B | CYCLE C |
|---------|---------|---------|
| Ex. 22:20-26 | Jer. 31:7-9 | Sir. 35:12-18 |
| Ps. 18:2-4,47,51 | Ps. 126:1-6 | Ps. 34:2-3,17-19,23 |
| 1 Thes. 1:5-10 | Heb. 5:1-6 | 2 Tm. 4:6-18 |
| Mt. 22:34-40 | Mk. 10:46-52 | Lk. 18:9-14 |

### -Thirty-first Sunday in Ordinary Time-

| CYCLE A | CYCLE B | CYCLE C |
|---------|---------|---------|
| Mal. 1:14—2:10 | Dt. 6:2-6 | Wis. 11:22—12:2 |
| Ps. 131:1-3 | Ps. 18:2-4,47,51 | Ps. 145:1-14 |
| 1 Thes. 2:7-13 | Heb. 7:23-28 | 2 Thes. 1:11—2:2 |
| Mt. 23:1-12 | Mk. 12:28-34 | Lk. 19:1-10 |

### -Thirty-second Sunday in Ordinary Time-

| CYCLE A | CYCLE B | CYCLE C |
|---------|---------|---------|
| Wis. 6:12-16 | 1 Kgs.17:10-16 | 2 Mc. 7:1-14 |
| Ps. 63:2-8 | Ps. 146:7-10 | Ps.17:1-15 |
| 1 Thes. 4:13-18 | Heb. 9:24-28 | 2 Thes. 2:16—3:5 |
| Mt. 25:1-13 | Mk. 12:38-44 | Lk. 20:27-38 |

### -Thirty-third Sunday in Ordinary Time-

| CYCLE A | CYCLE B | CYCLE C |
|---------|---------|---------|
| Prv. 31:10-31 | Dan. 12:1-3 | Mal. 3:19-20 |
| Ps. 128:1-5 | Ps. 16:5-11 | Ps. 98:5-9 |
| 1 Thes. 5:1-6 | Heb. 10:11-18 | 2 Thes. 3:7-12 |
| Mt. 25:14-30 | Mk. 13:24-32 | Lk. 21:5-19 |

### -Solemnity of Christ the King-
#### (last Sunday in Ordinary Time)

| CYCLE A | CYCLE B | CYCLE C |
|---------|---------|---------|
| Ez. 34:11-17 | Dan. 7:13-14 | 2 Sm. 5:1-3 |
| Ps. 23:1-6 | Ps. 93:1-2,5 | Ps. 122:1-5 |
| 1 Cor. 15:20-28 | Rv. 1:5-8 | Col. 1:12-20 |
| Mt. 25:31-46 | Jn. 18:33-37 | Lk. 23:35-43 |